what
economists
do

what economists do

ROBBIN R. HOUGH
Oakland University

HARPER & ROW, PUBLISHERS
New York
Evanston
San Francisco
London

TO THOSE STUDENTS
FROM WHOSE TOLERANCE FOR
OUTRAGEOUS IDEAS
SPRINGS HOPE

WHAT ECONOMISTS DO

Standard Book Number: 06-042915-1

Library of Congress
Catalog Card Number: 75-170619

What you are about to read is, as best as I can recall it,
the way an introductory economics course went one
recent summer when all of the students passed the course.
It is not a volume meant only to be read. It is a volume
to be discussed and felt. By "feel," I mean that its
ideas should be tried out in various ways much as one
hefts a rock to be thrown or scratches critical portions
of his anatomy.

The book, as faculty readers will soon note, departs
substantially from the usual outline under which introductory
economics texts are written and many introductory
courses are taught. The book was written on the major
premise that students must grasp and use a few
fundamental methodological concepts of economics if
further study in the field is to be rewarding. Therefore, an
attempt is made to place primary emphasis on *thinking*
with the "facts" at hand, and a serious attempt is made
to reduce the usual vocabulary requirements by an order
of magnitude.

The purpose of the book is, then, to lead the student to
the point where he or she may try on the economist's
shoes for size and become a doer rather than only a reader
of what has been done. In the author's experience, the
student's first steps are often quite awkward, but most
eventually manage to produce and test simple models of
decision-making behavior based on the approach
suggested here.

The first four chapters deal with a discussion of the
strategy of the volume, the development of descriptions of
decision makers, and the building of simple mathematical

models from these descriptions. The last three chapters
are aimed at helping the student confront the literature of
economics on his own.

The writer would like to thank his friends, neighbors, and
colleagues for their patience and assistance through what
could only appear to have been a most difficult "intellectual
pregnancy." Perhaps Edward Starr will find in this
volume something of the "output specifications" that he
so wisely sought for the introductory course in economics.
I am most grateful to John Tower and John Hurd for their
thoughtful and responsive critiques of the manuscript in
its various stages. Elutherios Botsas and Theodore Yntema
have surely served as articulate and responsive models.

My profound thanks are also due to Oakland University,
the U.S. Office of Education (for supporting some of my
research under Project 7-E-063), and Norton Seeber for
various forms of assistance of an "environmental
maintenance" sort. Mark Pachla's unerring sense of
direction was largely responsible for the form and inclusion
of Chapter 7.

My wife, Carol, and my chief competitors for her expert
and bountiful assistance, Whitney Eric and Tor, I thank
for their love and integrity.

I alone am responsible for the errors and any misguided
advice that may remain.

R.R.H.

contents

1

economists:
a systems
perspective

In the pages that follow, a set of ideas that economists have found to be very useful in the study of the world around them will be presented. If the reader possesses sufficient determination to grapple with the ideas set forth, he or she will be able to apply a specific set of concepts to everyday experiences. Therefore, the simplest way in which to provide the reader with a glimpse of what the book is about is to look briefly at the kind of final exam which a course involving this book might suggest.

Suppose that the book and/or instructor using the book had been successful in helping the student develop a firm grasp of the important concepts in the book. An appropriate final examination might be to ask the student to read an article from the *Wall Street Journal,* one of the journals of the economics profession, or some other socioeconomic annal, or a portion of a novel. Having read the piece, the reader would be asked to

(1) Identify the decision makers according to the way in which they are defined in Chapter 2.

(2) Build a simple algebraic or geometric "model" that caricatures the behavior of one of the decision makers after the fashion discussed in Chapter 3.

(3) Derive and verify the correctness of simple propositions about the expected behavior of the decision maker in responding to his environment.*

At the point when the reader is able to *do* these three things, the goal of this volume will have been reached. In order to reach that point it will be necessary to introduce the reader to the economists' peculiar use of the words of the English language. As the reader will come to under-

---

*A hypothesis is a proposition assumed as a premise in an argument. In economics, the argument usually takes the form of an algebraic or geometric model, and the hypothesis is subject to verification by reference to statistical evidence.

stand, the economist uses words in a fashion that might
seem distorted to some censorious observers.

Words usually have meaning only in terms of the context
in which they are found. If, for example, the reader
encounters the word *chimney,* he appreciates that there are
distinctions in its meaning that depend on whether the
writer is referring to the chimney of a house, a rock
chimney, or a heavy smoker. It can be said that the words
that economists use are almost never used in a context
familiar to the lay reader. A most embarrassing barrier to
communication is thus erected between the economist
and the lay reader. Each of the economist's words takes
on a "double meaning." The economist says the words
from one point of view, or in one context, and the reader
hears them in quite another.

The words used by the economist derive their meaning
from a context alien to the lay reader; this context derives
its meaning from a set of—largely unwritten—rules called a
methodology. As they write of the particular matters that
they study, economists do not attempt to convey parts of
the context; that is, they do not attempt to convey to the
reader the methodology (rules for thinking) within which
they write. It is, therefore, incumbent upon the reader to
somehow acquire that methodology for himself
through analysis and reasoning.

The relationship between the methodology and the
results of the writings of the economist may be seen by
observing certain parallels between the work of the
economist and the work of the artist. To produce a painting,
an artist must have a number of ideas about what he
seeks to accomplish and a set of guidelines to direct the
carrying out of the work. These ideas may be expressed,
for example, in terms of form, color, texture, and technique
—qualities that can be seen and identified by the knowl-
edgeable viewer. The concepts that guided the artist's

brush, however, are never immediately apparent to the beholder of the final work.

The ideas directing and guiding the artist's work are his methodology and they clearly differ from the final product of his efforts. The economist has both a set of concepts by which he expresses that which he seeks to accomplish and a set of guidelines for their use. That "basic set of tools" is precisely his methodology. Just as the concepts guiding the artist's brush are not immediately apparent in the final work, the concepts guiding the economist are seldom spelled out in the final statement of his work (an economics article or book).

Because the economist's methodology is seldom spelled out, it is necessary for the hapless reader to "fill in the blanks" with "words" from his own experience, or lack of experience, with the methodology of economics. Thus, a second way of stating the purpose of this volume is as follows: It will attempt to spell out to the reader something about how economists think and suggest ways in which the reader may gain some experience with the economist's brand of thinking.

There are in fact two quite distinct "languages" that professional economists use. They share a general "language of science" with other scientific disciplines. In addition, the historical development of economic thought has produced a very powerful and useful language peculiar to economics. The learning of either of these languages is a difficult but rewarding task.

A one-semester course in a university is perhaps just long enough to allow the reader to develop a halting command of one of the two. For that reason, this volume is primarily concerned with one of these languages. For purposes that will soon become clear, the second of the two languages has been chosen as the primary focus of study. However, before turning our concentration to the second language, it is important to at least briefly make the connection between the language of economics and the more general "language of science."

THE LANGUAGE OF SCIENCE

For the solution of many problems, *all* scientists have found it helpful to use the idea of a *black box.* The scientist views himself as possessing a black box that is closed to his inspection, but into which he may put things, and out of which other things will come. He perceives the task of studying an animal, stream, economy, chemical reaction, or other complex phenomena as determining (a) just which inputs are taken in by the "black box," (b) what the black box does with those inputs, and (c) what outputs are produced by the black box.

There are countless simple physical examples of such black boxes that convert inputs (the things that go in) into outputs (the things that come out). The reader will find it useful to consider several simple examples and then go on to develop a list of his own examples in order to get the ideas firmly in mind. Jukeboxes and candy machines (black boxes) convert coins and button selections (inputs) into music and candy bars (outputs). The ideas in this book will serve as inputs to the reader (black box) who will convert them into insight, humor, boredom, interest, or whatever (outputs).

The use of the idea of the black box and the many concepts (input and output here) which are related to that use is called the *systems* approach.

Economists, in particular, have found systems ideas to be an indispensable aid to the description and prediction of the behavior of economies as a whole. Macroeconomics, as it is called, is devoted almost exclusively to the study of the economy from the systems point of view.

Varying choices for the spending of money (inputs) are looked upon as bringing about the production of a wide variety of goods and services (outputs). The relationship between investment spending (input) and the growth in goods produced is sought. The relationship between inflation (one output) and unemployment (another output) is studied.

A greatly oversimplified view of a current problem will serve to illustrate the way in which input, black box, and output may be used to examine important and complex phenomena. Consider, for example, the following description of the "pollution" problem. Using the systems perspective, the *economic system* might be described as a black box that converts spending by individuals, corporations, and governmental bodies into goods, services, and pollution. Thus, for each level of spending by these groups (input) there will be a corresponding level of pollution (output). A complimentary description of the *ecological system* might observe that each level of pollution (input) in the economic system brings about a corresponding death rate (output) in the ecological system. The *social system* might be depicted as monitoring death rates in the ecological system (inputs) and, for each death death rate observed, producing a corresponding level of protest (output). Finally, a responsive *political system* might be depicted as the conversion of protest levels (inputs) into tax levels on spending (outputs).

Figure 1.1 illustrates the way in which the four systems of the previous paragraph interact. It is to be noted that the inputs of each are shown to be the outputs of one of the other systems. Those with a little background in algebra will, of course, recognize that such a set of interacting systems might also be described by a set of four simultaneous equations. Within this broad view, it is easy to see some of the many ways in which

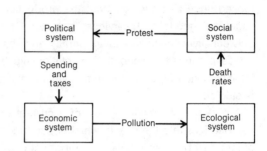

Figure 1.1
Interacting
Systems

the same ideas might help scientists from many disciplines
contribute to our understanding of the pollution problem.

An economist might attempt to understand the particular
ways in which changes in spending result in changes in
the level of pollution. He might look at total spending and
total pollution or the varieties of pollution produced by a
particular type of spending. He might look at the pollution
produced by the spending for the products of certain
industries (black boxes), regions (black boxes), or firms
(black boxes).

An ecologist could approach the problems of the effects
of pollution on the various forms of life in a similar fashion.
He might choose a stream, forest, or city as a black box.
Specific pollutants might be studied as inputs and the
effects of pollutants on specific life forms could be classified
as outputs. Depending on the black box chosen, the
special technical skills used by virtually any of the natural
sciences may be required by the investigator. The
following hypothetical titles or study topics illustrate the
idea: the physiological effects of trace mineral inputs on
the life span of rabbits; the effects of phosphate fertilizers
on the chemical balance of a stream; the toxicologic effects
of sustained sulphur dioxide intake on human lungs;
particulate size and the effusion of pollution; water

temperature and the reproduction cycle of salmon; and aromatic traces and the behavior of insect populations.

Sociologists, social psychologists, and other interested social scientists have been studying, for some time now, the various forms of organized social protest. Numerous forms (outputs) have been studied in some detail. They include strikes, boycotts, work slowdowns, sit-ins, lobbying, write-in and telephone campaigns, impeachment attempts, and many others. The protest output would probably depend upon the black box studies—unions, social clubs, patriotic organizations, firms, tribes, and religious organizations—as well as on the level of the "death" input.

Finally, the linkage between protest and spending or sanctions on spending is, at least in part, a political one. The connections between protest forms (inputs) and tax levels, subsidy levels, legal prohibitions, political patronage, the distribution of government expenditures, the distribution of government services, or tax assessments are, therefore, likely to interest the political scientist.

Now, it will come as no surprise to the reader that, in order to simplify the discussion of the black boxes under study, scientists have developed a range of additional concepts. It may be said that an entire *language* of science has been produced, the terms of which are used to discuss black boxes. *Feedback* describes the situation in which an output of a black box is used as an input for the same black box. *Imports* and *exports* are terms used to describe those inputs that are given to the black box by its environment and the outputs sent out to its environment. *Negative entropy* describes the complexity with which the black box is believed to be ordered. Scientists distinguish between *information inputs* and *energy inputs.* Further discussion of the development of this language is beyond the scope of the present topic. It is, however, of great importance for the reader to observe that the concepts named have no meaning outside of their use in the description and study of black boxes. That is, if one is trying to think about some portion of reality *as if* it were a black box, these concepts used together will aid the individual in the organization of his thoughts. Thus, if the firm is thought of as a black box, customer reactions to advertising may be thought of as providing "feedback." If a stream is thought of as a black box, chemical inputs will react with the chemical elements in the stream until an "equilibrium" is reached. The sun provides not only "energy inputs" to plants, but also "information inputs" designed to cause the plants to grow in the direction of the sun (output).

If these terms are used to "translate what is said," some sense can be made of otherwise impossible utterances of scientists at work on esoteric problems. Consider a pair of examples. Without benefit of the black box concepts, a title such as "Cellulosic Wall Components Produced by the Gogli Apparatus of Pleurochrisis Scherffelli" reads like a wild phrase from Dr. Suess. Yet, within the Pleurochrisis Scherffelli (black box) there may be another black box called a Gogli Apparatus, and the Gogli Apparatus may produce Cellulosic Wall Components (outputs)—whatever they are. The pharmacologists who wrote "Anti-Parkinsonian Drugs: Inhibition of Dopamine Uptake in the Corpus Stratium as a Possible Mechanism of Action" had no intention of reaching the bedside table of folk other than pharmacologists. However, some lay reader may find reassurance in the notion that the Corpus Stratium may be thought of as a black box whose Dopamine Intake (inputs) may be inhibited by inputs of certain Anti-Parkinsonian Drugs.

As considered in the previous paragraphs, all sciences share the same language. Biologists, crystalographers, and economists are all concerned with the "growth" processes. Chemists, engineers, and economists are concerned with the "equilibrium" of their various systems. However, only part of the work done in any of the disciplines can be understood in terms of the systems language. Though the language may be used fruitfully in the investigation of many interesting problems, each of the disciplines has vitally— or considerably—important other languages (or collections of related concepts).

Indeed, the widespread use of the black box perspective is a rather recent phenomenon in the development of economics. Until the advent of macroeconomics in the 1930s and 1940s, the primary advances in economic thought centered on insights into the actions of decision makers. As a result, most of the work done in economics freely draws upon those concepts developed in the study of decision-making entities (microeconomics). The remainder of this book is, therefore, devoted to a discussion of various possible ways of thinking about decision makers, or *institutions* as they will be called.*

The "language" developed may be looked upon as complementing the black box language in use. That is, if progress in the study of a decision maker is halted, the economist may adopt the black box language in order to move forward again. Though "doing economics" must ultimately involve mastery of both languages, the historical development described above gives the language used to study decision makers an independence in economics not enjoyed by the black box language *as used* by economists. In effect, economists cannot ignore their knowledge of what goes on inside the black box, even when they would like to.

---

*As used in this volume the terms "decision maker" and "institution" will be used interchangeably.

ECONOMICS AS A WAY OF THINKING ABOUT DECISION MAKERS

The next several chapters of this volume will treat the *economist himself* as a black box. The inputs to the economist are of two types. The first of these inputs are verbal descriptions of decision makers, or, as they will be called, *institutional descriptions*. The second type of input consists of numerical descriptions, or, as they will be called, *statistical descriptions.* What goes on inside the black box is a process resulting in a comparison of an institutional description with a statistical description. That process involves two steps. In the first step, the institutional descriptions are placed in a form comparable to the statistical descriptions. That form is called an *institutional model.* In the second step, certain parts, called hypotheses, of the institutional model are compared with the statistical description in order to test the adequacy of the institutional model. The output of the black box is the *literature of economics.*

To repeat and expand slightly, the economist's study of decision makers proceeds according to a relatively simple process. First, certain limited observations are made about the world (institutional description). Second, those descriptions are converted into collections of statements about the relationships among the words in the description (institutional model). Third, another set of observations about the world is collected (statistical description). Next, the relationships observed to hold among the words in the statistical description are compared with the relationships said to hold in the model in order to make possible the acceptance or rejection of the model. Parts of the process are described, and the results are often recorded in the formal literature of economics.

The remainder of this volume is concerned with assisting the reader in the development of a sufficient grasp of the

process so that he will be able to "do" a little
economic thinking about decision makers. In Chapter 2
institutional descriptions will be defined and the reader
will be invited to try his hand at constructing his
own descriptions. In Chapter 3 the process by which
institutional models are fashioned from institutional
descriptions will be examined so that the reader will be
able to build simple models of decision-making behavior.
In Chapter 4 the concepts used to verify hypotheses
concerning behavior will be discussed. Finally, the last
three chapters will introduce readers to various uses to
which their new ideas may be put.

THE REWARDS OF LEARNING

Implementing the strategy suggested will require considerable effort on the part of the reader. It is fair that he
be given some idea of the potential rewards that
can be derived from that effort. Economic thought, as it
relates to the study of decision makers, provides a
systematic means for acquiring a *new perspective* on the
relations between individuals and/or certain groups of
individuals. Should readers come to understand, in some
degree, how economists think, they should be able to
use that understanding to develop new ways in which to
look at themselves and others as individuals or groups of
individuals. As a means of making it possible to identify
the active agents in an environment, such an ability is
important in and of itself.

But, it is all very well to assert that at some future point
a particular effort will pay off in one way or another. How,
in fact, will that payoff be seen by an individual? From
the experience of the writer there are several ways in
which it will be felt.

First, like "black box thinking," economic thought

provides a range of fairly precise questions. These questions may be asked again and again in different contexts. Thus, just as the reader will find that economics professors have an irritating tendency to answer one question by asking another one, the reader will find that as he acquires an understanding of the economist's way of thinking, he will begin to ask the same types of questions. The questions raised will often deal contentiously with widely accepted "facts." Similarly, some of our pet theories will fail to withstand elementary tests of their validity.

Second, economic thought provides the economist, and thus, potentially, the reader, with a way of knowing when to quit when the approach adopted has either succeeded, or failed and must therefore be discarded. Insofar as an explanation fails to survive a test of its validity, it demands that the user cast out the explanation. Thus, rather than continue to hammer away at a problem from an inadequate perspective, the economist learns when to withdraw and reconsider his approach.

Finally, insofar as one is able to generate new per-spectives from which to view other problems, one may learn to step outside of oneself and view one's own behavior somewhat more objectively. In short, economics as a way of thinking can assist the individual in freeing himself from a single point of view.

2

institutional
descriptions

Economists use only a limited set of terms to describe the world as it relates to their studies of decision makers. In the present chapter the classes of words in that vocabulary will be described. That is the central purpose of the chapter. However, before proceeding too far, it is important to gain a perspective on what it is that the economist is trying to accomplish.

The goal of the economist is simply to predict the behavior of individuals and certain of the groups (institutions) into which they gather. The word *predict* is not very popular in many quarters. It reeks of charlatans and soothsayers or, even worse in the context of current values, social engineers. As commonly used, predictions weave the fabric of credibility gaps. As used here, the term means nothing more than a reduction in the surprise experienced by the observer as he watches the results of social interaction. Thus, if an observer were aware that a football team was allowed to punt after the third down, he would be less surprised than an uninformed counterpart when the subsequent kick occurred at the appropriate time. The process of prediction is, in a very real sense, a search for the unwritten rules of a game.

From the cocktail party to the corporation, our civilization has produced a bewildering array of "people groups" with which individuals and other groups must interact. A reader of the literature of economics would conclude that economists have attempted to predict the behavior of a relatively small number of these groups. An abbreviated list of the "heavies" in economists' melodramas would include consumers, firms, governments, banks, workers, trade unions, and entreprenuers. It is an easily taken, but simply mistaken, step to conclude that economics *is* the study of these groups. By considering only those groups studied in the past, one loses sight of economics as a way of thinking about more general matters.

If the behavior of an individual is to be predicted, it is important to know which *elements of his response* to a situation are related directly or indirectly to *elements of the situation itself.* Most individuals have *well-integrated* personalities; that is, they only slightly alter their personalities in response to the demands of a particular situation. An individual's conversation with members of his family will differ somewhat from a conversation with his peers or employers in matters such as, for example, X-rated movies. In few cases is it found that behavior changes so dramatically from one encounter to another that the person literally changes his identity. From the systems perspective, similar encounters (inputs) with other people will usually produce similar, and therefore predictable, responses (outputs) in the individual.

In dealing with groups, it is not always the case that similar inputs will yield reliably similar outputs. In a particular class of such groups, however, similar inputs do yield similar outputs. It is on those groups that economists have concentrated. The groups are sometimes called *decision-making groups,* or *institutions,* see p. 11.

The word *institution* as it will be used throughout this volume refers, then, to a locus of decision making. This definition would, at first glance, seem to conflict with sociologists' traditional usage. Sociologists refer to institutions as "firmly established and structured patterns of behavior" that are accepted as basic parts of a culture such as marriage, the family, slavery, and so on. The similarities between economists' and sociologists' usage will soon be seen to outweigh any apparent conflict. While the sociologist would presumably prefer not to apply the word *institution* to individuals, both the sociologist's definition and the definition given here focus on *the transfer of some decision-making responsibility from the individual to an aggregation of at least two individuals of which the first is a member.* The usage adopted here simply insists that the aggregation be *defined* very carefully in terms to be discussed below.

The chief problem encountered in attempting to isolate proper institutions lies in the fact that there are so many collections of individuals that would appear to be institutions. The sheer weight of numbers could easily distract our analytic energies. For the purpose of a particular problem, a group of individuals may fail to qualify as an institution. Cocktail parties, yellow hordes, military-industrial complexes, and establishments of many types may or may not qualify for the label. Consider the issue further.

WHO?

When is a university an institution? There will always be commencement speakers who proclaim the highest ideals of education. But when does the label "university" simply serve to mask the identity of a number of warring institu- tions (student, faculty, and administrative coalitions) who have chosen a particular piece of geographic or intellectual real estate on which to conduct their campaigns? Is there a "military-industrial complex," or are we viewing—through slightly paranoid eyes—the interaction of a number of small but identifiable groups pursuing their own interests unchecked? How many social welfare organizations have degenerated into noninstitutions in terms of their professed goals? Many seem incapable of operating on the poverty or civil rights fronts. In spite of glossy brochures to the contrary, is their behavior predictable only in terms of the individuals who make them up?

In each case it is a matter of importance that an institution be correctly perceived. Consider a minor but useful example. Universities tend to offer two types of courses: large lecture courses, with few prerequisites, comprising about one-half of a student's required course load, and small discussion courses designed for upper-level students in their particular major fields. The total enrollment (and thus the fees collected) in the university may at times depend on the care with which the large "requirement filling" courses are mixed with smaller courses for the major. Often the budgets of individual departments are determined by a headcount of the students enrolled in their courses for a given term. It thus behooves a department to offer a good many "requirement filling" courses as these will fill large lecture halls to the glory and honor of the department concerned. If all departments were to behave in the same way and offer only the large general education courses, the number of upper-level students in attendance would be quite likely to fall off dramatically. It is the way in which small problems such as this are solved that may ultimately help to distinguish between universities and collections of departments. If the university is an institution, the courses are likely to be scheduled so that overall university attendance is as high as possible when funding depends on enrollment. In effect, some departments sacrifice for the greater good. In a university where institutions are found only at the department level, a diversity of upper-division courses will be forgone in favor of a larger headcount for some departments.

Those elements of a situation that will assist in under-standing where decision making takes place must be isolated. The economist uses three questions to help him discern who is involved. He asks of each potential institution: "What are you trying to do?" or "What is your *goal*?"; "How do you intend to reach your goal?" or "What are your *instruments*?"; and "What factors—beyond your

immediate control—will help or hinder your attempt to
reach your goal?" or "What are the *intervening variables*?"
These questions will be examined in turn.

The prediction of decision-making behavior requires either
knowledge of what the institution is trying to accomplish
or a willingness to make explicit assumptions about what
it is trying to accomplish. Having observed a sign on a
passing bus or having asked the driver of a passing
car where he is going, it is possible for an observer to
make a reasonable prediction as to where one might find
the bus or the car after an appropriate period of time has
passed. Though the task of defining the goals of a
potential institution seems simple enough on the surface,
it is generously endowed with emotional, if not analytical,
difficulties.

It is precisely at the point of defining the goals of the
institution that meaning, in the context of everyday
experience, departs substantially from meaning in the
context of institutional model building. At this point in the
narrative two short-range goals may be reached. First, it
will bo possible to shed some light on why the break
occurs, and second, it will also be possible to suggest just
a little about the nature of the break.

Were a budding Adam Smith to take to the floor at a
cocktail party and yell "What is your goal?" he would,
at the very least, be met by some strange looks. By the
same token, should he write to the public relations office
of a major business firm and ask "What are you trying
to do?" he would shortly receive an impressive document
containing pledges of fealty to such worthies as mother,
God, the consumer, and, most especially, the
stockholder. The small businessman would reply to a

similar question in terms of customer service, a good life
for his family, an education for his children, a pleasant
working place for his employees, and so on. And, in fact,
these people would be telling the truth—because their
replies would be made within the context of their frames
of reference.

It is tempting, therefore, to say that the cocktail party
is a noninstitution or collection of institutions and that the
business firm is an institution and let it go at that. Unfortunately, experience is a cruel taskmaster. To refer to
the previous discussion of the university, "the university"
may not even exist as a meaningful decision-making unit
and yet it may continue to issue statements espousing
noble goals. In fact, the economist has given up in his
attempts to get helpful answers to the question "What is
your goal?" Of course, a group's willingness to answer
the question may be an indication that it would like to be
an institution. Its answer, however, is still *not* acceptable
evidence that it is one.

Instead of asking the question directly, the economist
asks himself "What does the potential institution *act as if*
it is trying to do?" In phrasing the question in this way,
he at once removes himself to an analytic plane and away
from long, heart-rending harangues at the institution
he studies.

However, these ideas about goals take some getting
used to. The economist characterizes firms as "profit
maximizers" and consumers as "utility maximizers." These
characterizations call forth, in many minds, visions of
greedy capitalists on the one hand and hell-bent hedonists
on the other. If care is not taken to understand what he
is saying, the economist's assumption can be twisted from
a useful and analytically powerful fiction to an unveiled
threat to humanism. The notion of "maximizing"
anything is meaningful only in the context of institutional

models, as will be seen in the next chapter. What matters
to the economist is the eventual prediction resulting from
his analytic efforts. Put another way, he is concerned with
the alternative perspective made possible by using the
admittedly fictional characterization. Often the modification
of the goal of an institution being studied has no impact
whatsoever on the prediction. To use the concept of
"happiness maximization," or "tenderness maximization,"
or a whole range of alternative constructs will fail to
change the resulting prediction, if the concept of utility
is always used in the sense that an economist uses it.
Hopefully, the reader will eventually become more
comfortable with this view.

Here, it is important to observe that the "potential
institution" must be treated as if it has a particular goal
and that the goal serves as the focus of the institution's
decision making.

HOW?

How does an institution try to reach its goals? What are
the actions that will propel it in the desired direction? When
an institution has defined its goals, the decision-making
process is reduced to the selection of the appropriate
means for achieving those goals. The *instruments* are the
actions and reactions of the institutions. The instruments
of a society's institutions are closely paralleled by the set
of transitive verbs available in the language spoken by
the society.

Institutions

I and you
must know that do
is what instruments are about.

Not in one ear
and on through clear,
but moved to loose a shout
that the transitive verbs
used from cities to slurbs
tell us what who do and are seeds
of a clear insight into who's might
—they focus on who's deeds.

By who's deeds who is known.
If no seeds who has sewn,
forget who—cause who can't exist.
But if who can do,
it will make sense for you
to label the acts which persist.

That means you must watch
'til you've labeled a clotch
of the actions that characterize
a who that's effective
at choices elective
and makes few that are otherwise.
As observed by the trade,
institutions are made
of folk who give up some free choices,
who put on a ring
or make group work their thing.
The result is a choir of voices.
Now a choir has troubles
if personal bubbles
continue to get in the way.
But if we are agreed
there is one special deed
they can do, then we say—
that an instrument's there,
the choir's aware,

may even exist—be defined.
So we look further on
and may find that anon
from this start a prediction's refined.

The reader, too, is an institution with a wide range of
instruments by which he or she will pursue chosen goals.
Without definable goals, an institution is unpredictable.
Without instruments, it is impotent. In either case it becomes
a noninstitution to the economist. Individuals have many
instruments. Institutions that involve "people groups" have
relatively few to move them toward a specified goal.

What, for example, can a university—as a university—
do? There is a long list of actions that individual members
of a university community can take. Compiling even a
short list of alternative courses of actions possible for a
collective community can be a very difficult task indeed.
Considerable cooperation among diverse subgroups
would be necessary to create the singleness of purpose
necessary; and, after that goal had been achieved, an
effective set of instruments for the entire community would
then be needed. Since the advent of the "multiversity,"
such cooperation has become increasingly difficult to
achieve in larger academic institutions. To understand their
behavior, it may, therefore, be necessary to treat competing
subgroups as institutions.

An institution is, thus, defined by its goals and by the
instruments it uses to pursue those goals. Without goals,
the institution is likely to be in hopeless, if not pathological,
confusion. Without instruments, its cause would be
considered hopeless, even if glorious. Though somewhat
"hardheaded," the depiction has the merit of focusing
on what was or is, rather than what might have been or
might be. The question of "what will be" thus becomes
somewhat easier to deal with.

WHEN AND WHERE?

It is necessary also to have some means of discussing the ways in which the environment and other institutions enhance or restrict the operations of the institution with which we are concerned. Institutions do not operate in a vacuum. They inhabit a particular environment containing resources and other institutions. In the same way that the actions of the institution are called *instruments,* the possible changes in its environment, including the instruments under the control of other institutions, will be called *intervening variables.*

Many intervening variables are probably important to the average college student. Consider these, for example: parent's income, sex, tuition levels, number of roommates, his or her academic ability, distance from home, class schedule, age, availability of a car, and so on. The corporation sees corporate income, taxes, prices of materials, transportation costs, wages, zoning restrictions, and a number of other intervening variables as crucial to its operations. The activities of a government are limited by the extent of the nation's natural resources, the political beliefs of its people, the rate of growth of its population, the skills of its labor force, the level of its technological development, and so forth. Similarly, other institutions have particular goals and instruments and will respond to changes in particular variables.

INSTITUTIONAL DESCRIPTIONS AS PREDICTIONS

The basic concepts that can be used to describe the economist as one who filters out irrelevant inputs are now in place. In the construction of institutional descriptions he is concerned primarily with the instruments, intervening variables, and goals that make it possible to define the decision-making group, or institution.

The provision of the appropriate institutional descriptions to view a particular problem may be seen as reaching a first basic level of predictive ability, so long as prediction is thought of as a reduction in the element of surprise. The chief way in which the reduction in surprise is brought about is through the development of an alternative point of view of the problem under consideration. Each new perspective produced brings about a concomitant reduction in surprise to the analyst—as long as some elements of that perspective are clearly visible in the situation under study. Consider a simple example in which the elements of the description may dramatically alter the point of view.

My typical reader—at this point in his academic career—has, in all probability, made at least a glancing acquaintance with various great historical events. Therefore, I am assuming that he has been subjected to one or more versions of the eleventh-century Crusades. The voracious Seljuq Turks, crumbling Byzantine Empire, and scheming ambitious Italian cities undoubtedly played a part in shaping one or two of those versions. The following explanation of the Crusades owes much to a group of students who found themselves "high" on the use of institutional descriptions.

Economics has often been called the "dismal science." One of the major reasons for this unhappy reputation is the observation by Reverend Robert Malthus that rates of population growth are inexorably related to fluctuations in agricultural output. Malthus may not have dealt with one of the more cheerful aspects of the human condition, but his observation may have been nonetheless correct— especially when seen in the context of his own times. While the reader is not yet ready to deal with all of the

whys and wherefores of the Malthusian prophecy, he
may appreciate the conclusion that medieval life
alternated between periods of plenty during which the
population would grow at very high rates and periods of
poverty during which the gains in population of the previous
period would be wiped out by starvation and disease.
Similarly, cycles of poverty and plenty also haunt such pred-
itors and prey of the natural domain as wolves and rabbits.

What, the reader may ask, has that to do with Crusades?
To which the response must be

    "What is a crusade?"

    "A crusade is a holy war."

    "Is it an institution, instrument, intervening variable,
or goal?"

    "An instrument."

    "An instrument in whose hands? What is the
institution?"

    "The Pope."

    "What was Urban's goal?"

    "To thrash the heathen infidels!"

    "Suppose, as will be suggested in a later chapter, that
it never pays for an institution to fight. What then
might be the goal?"

    "Hard to say."

    "Suppose that you were a medieval baron living an
increasingly modest castle existence because of
dwindling tax revenues, crop failures, and increasing
numbers of highwaymen on the paths of your barony.
Suppose further that word had reached you of an uprising
about to take place among the peasants. The peasants
are beginning to starve (as the Malthusian doctrine
would have it), but as a token of more prosperous times
they outnumber you and the nobility by about 50 to 1.
You are there, what do you do?"

"Put down the rebellion."

"Since you are hopelessly outnumbered," said the economist, "why not send them on a crusade? If they are allowed to say where they are, the situation can only fester and lead to greater trouble. However, if you can give them a good and noble cause, promise them everlasting life and 10 percent of the take, they may even send their children. Your major problem will be to find a sufficiently zealous nobleman to lead them—one who, at the same time, will agree to let you stay home and divide the spoils among the fewer remaining mouths."

THINKING ABOUT CHAPTER 2

To some, the four words on which this chapter has dwelled will seem simple and obvious. To others, the chapter may seem vague and mysterious. It can be said that unless the reader now takes the time to think about and apply these four concepts, his efforts thus far will have been for nothing.

One way in which the reader may expand the meaning of these terms is to view himself as an institution and then apply the terms to himself. Such an application, of course, would involve a cataloging of the reader's instruments and goals. It should also include a cataloging of the instruments and goals of the institutions with which the reader interacts. In the next several paragraphs a few illustrative institutional descriptions will be set forth, each of which might apply to a college or university student as an institution.

Consider the overweight student who jogs (instrument) in order to lose weight (goal). The intervening variables relevant to such an institutional description might include the temperature, the humidity, the prevailing variations in elevation in the area where he jogs, his physical condition, and the activities that he must forgo (his *opportunity cost*). Changes in each of the intervening variables would determine—at least in part—the extent to which his instrument would be utilized.

Consider the student who is attempting to obtain a good job (goal) by maintaining a high grade-point average (intervening variable). Properly mixed, there are many instruments available to such a student. Dating, physical exercise, study, the seeking of counsel, working, and thinking may each contribute to the attainment of that goal. The person's physical and mental condition and the instruments of his instructors and peers would surely be included among the intervening variables.

As a final example, consider the reader's attempts to work his way through this volume. The reader is reading (instrument), let us say, to maximize utility. There are a set of intervening variables about which the reader has probably not thought. These variables may be called *word associations*. Except under rare circumstances, attempts by an individual to read or listen are interrupted from time to time by stray thoughts about sports, sex, family, work, friends, or other matters of current importance to the individual. So it is as the reader proceeds through this volume. Seemingly innocent words that have been used in a particular context will trigger thoughts about matters alien to the volume being read or the subject matter of a lecture being listened to.

A second approach to expanding the meaning of the four terms is that of applying them to the output of reporters, news commentators, writers, and so on. Who are the institutions of which they write and speak? What are the instruments and intervening variables? Which are the goals? Care must be exercised or the reader will be found cataloging the trivia of the world. The newsstand catalog of late movies can provide a look at the problem of "descriptive pathology." The zealous user of institutional descriptions will note instantly that the titles to nearly every movie ever made may be placed in an orderly classification according to whether or not the movie title refers to an institution *(The Barefoot Executive* or *The Brotherhood of Satan)*, an instrument variable *(Claire's Knee)*, collections of instrument variables *(A New Leaf)*, a goal *(Making It)*, or collections of intervening variables *(Tora Tora* or *Zeppelin)*. Some titles, of course, provide more ambitious descriptions which include several classes of terms. *Valdez Is Coming* suggests that an institution has an instrument. *Say Hello to Yesterday* demands that the watcher be able to greet the past. *Investigation of a Citizen Above Suspicion* indicates that one institution will exercise the instrument of investigation toward another institution (the citizen) who has the intervening variable that he could not be thought of as suspicious. An imaginative reader can doubtlessly find other areas in which the use of these terms will yield results quite as trivial as those above.

Without regard to where these concepts are applied, there are several rules that will prove useful in guiding the reader's efforts.

First, an institution can *never* be an instrument. Since institutions are decision makers possessing their own instruments, intervening variables, and goals, the depiction of them as instruments or intervening variables leads to analytic difficulty. Thus, a university interacts with students and faculty who are not the instruments of the university. Rather, the students' instruments must be considered the intervening variables to which the university may react (if it exists).

Second, the list of instruments that an institution *may* have is roughly delimited by the list of verbs possible in sentences in which the institution is the subject.

A third useful rule to follow relates to the treatment of things. It is the properties of things that are important and not the things themselves. Thus, the speed, comfort, sail area, freeboard, availability, and other characteristics of a sailboat are important. The properties of things will be intervening variables for a decision maker and not the things themselves.

With these several hints in mind, the reader will, we hope, spend a number of hours improving his ability to deal with institutional descriptions.

3

institutional
models

The completion of an institutional description only brings the economist one step closer to understanding the behavior of the institution to which it applies. Having observed that an institution possesses certain instruments, or that it must take into account particular intervening variables, the economist is, presumably, much less startled when he sees the institution use those instruments or react to changes in those intervening variables.

To assert that an individual *can* jump is not to say that the individual *will* jump if poked; nor can we know how far or in what direction. One qualitative improvement in understanding is represented by the ability to specify that there is a relation between two variables (jump and poke). A second qualitative improvement is possible in specifying the direction of the effect of one variable on the other (in which direction). Finally, a relatively complete specification of the relationship between two variables will include a statement of the probable magnitude of the effect of one variable on the other. By an obvious convention, the variable changed by another variable is called the *dependent variable* (jump). The variable whose value determines, at least in part, the value of the dependent variable is called the *independent variable* (poke).

The chief business of institutional model building is the translation of institutional descriptions into more precise statements about the existence, magnitude, and direction of the effects of variables (instrument variables and intervening variables) upon one another. The attempts of the economist to define qualitatively the relationships between variables is called *theorizing,* or *model building.*

An institutional model is a collection of "expressions" relating instruments, intervening variables, and goals. The primary concern of the present chapter will be the development of a means for expressing those hypotheses

that concern the response of an institution to changes
in the value of its intervening variables.

CONSTRUCTION OF A MODEL

The following scenario will serve as the focus for the study
of how hypotheses are derived. Suppose that a fortunate
explorer were to discover a mineral spring with miraculous
curative powers. Suppose further that the explorer has
been supported in his searches by a king who intends to
recover his outlays for the venture by levying a tax on
each cup of mineral water that the explorer-producer sells
to the single surviving subject of the king. These are the
basic ingredients of an endlessly recurring problem in
economics; the simple model that may be used to analyze
the problem will be seen to have many useful applications
well beyond its original domain.

Consider, first, the institutional description of the problem.
There are three institutions: the king, the explorer-producer,
and the subject. Each has an instrument. The king may
set the level of the tax in cents per cup. The producer may
determine the price of the cup, and the king's subject may
decide how much mineral water he will buy. The instruments
of each pair will appear as intervening variables to the
third. The consumer derives utility (or satisfaction) from
the consumption of the water. His goal may therefore be
expressed in terms of utility. The producer receives
revenues from the sale of the water and the king receives
tax revenues from the tax levied. The goals of the latter
two institutions may therefore be expressed in terms of
their revenue desires.

A means of expressing the relations between utility and
the water bought, revenue and the water sold, and the
level of the tax and tax revenues now becomes necessary.

A convenient method for the expression of those relationships is found in *functional notation.*

The relationship between the subject's utility and output may be stated as $U = f(Q)$, where utility is an index of satisfaction and output *(Q)* is a measure of the quantity consumed. In plain English, utility is a function of the level of consumption. Alternatively, the expression may be interpreted as stating that for every level of Q there is a corresponding level of U.

In order to get the idea firmly in mind, it is useful to refer again to the idea of a system. In earlier discussions a system was viewed as a black box transforming inputs into outputs. The expression $U = f(Q)$ may also be interpreted as a simple statement of a system in which Q is the input and U is the output. In such an interpretation $f(\ )$ may be thought of as simply being a black box. By convention again, the input is usually referred to as the independent variable and the output as the dependent variable.

The basic set of expressions relating the instruments of the three institutions to their goals may thus be stated as follows:

$$U = f(Q) \tag{3.1}$$
$$R = f(Q) \tag{3.2}$$
$$T = f(Q) \tag{3.3}$$

where R is the total revenue of the producer and T is the total tax revenue collected by the king. In Equation 3.1, Q refers to the quantity consumed. In Equation 3.2, Q refers to the quantity produced. In Equation 3.3, Q refers to the quantity produced.

Pause and note well the usefulness of the idea of a function. It provides a highly flexible way of expressing the relationship between possibly significant variables. In the form stated above, the function simply asserts the *existence* of a relationship. Another form of function may be used to describe exactly what goes on inside the black box. Thus, the expression $Q = a - bT^2$ tells us that the black box squares T, multiplies that result by a constant b, and subtracts that product from a constant a in order to produce Q. The reader should verify that in the particular case where $a = 2$, $b = 3$, and $T = 4$, the value of Q is -46. For each value of T, of course, a different value of Q would result.

THE CONCEPT OF EQUILIBRIUM

To improve upon the earlier definition, an institutional model is a collection of *functions* relating instruments, intervening variables, and goals. It is assembled so as to describe an institution's *equilibrium* with its environment. There is an abundance of physical and biological analogies that may be used to illustrate the general idea of an equilibrium model.

A falcon that is momentarily buoyed up by a current of warm air just exactly strong enough to support his weight may be said to be in equilibrium for just that brief period of time. The expression describing that equilibrium would express the equality of the upward force of air and the downward pull of gravity. The swinging door on an old western barroom returning to its normal state after the villain has been thrown out can be said to be searching for its equilibrium. That equilibrium would be defined in terms of the equal opposing forces of the springs when the door is at rest. An orbiting satellite finds an equilibrium based on the equality of the pull of gravity and the centrifugal force tending to hurl the satellite into outer space.

A somewhat more sophisticated set of equilibriums are found in the biological domain. In these processes equilibrium "growth rates" for living organisms are determined by much more complex interactions of opposing forces.

In the set of equations describing the producer, the consumer, and the king, equilibrium may be said to occur when the quantity bought is equal to the quantity produced and the king is satisfied with his tax revenues. In order to reach a statement of that equilibrium, it is necessary to be able to provide hypotheses about the reaction of each of the institutions to changes in its intervening variables. In order to reach a conclusion about the overall equilibrium, or *general equilibrium,* it is useful, therefore, to consider each institution individually while assuming the behavior of the other two institutions to be held constant. This approach is called *partial equilibrium* analysis.

Partial Equilibrium Analysis

Figure 3.1 shows graphically a relationship assumed to exist between the utility received per unit of mineral water consumed by the consumer and the total units consumed by him. The solid line, labeled P_1, simply asserts that as the consumer uses more and more mineral water in a given time period, the utility that he receives from each unit consumed declines until, at Q_1, he is overfull and receives no utility at all.

At any point such as X on the "utility function" the box enclosed by the axes and the dashed lines is a measure of the total utility received by the consumer. For each such point there is a particular box of a specific size.

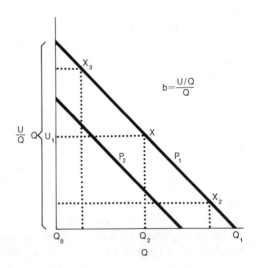

Figure 3.1
A Simple
Utility Function

The boxes corresponding to points X_2 and X_3 are obviously smaller in area than the box corresponding to X_1. In fact, an examination of the sizes of the boxes corresponding to increasing levels of consumption from Q_0 to Q_1 will indicate that the boxes grow larger until the level Q_2 is reached and that they become successively smaller after that point is reached.

If the consumer seeks the greatest level of utility attainable by him, he would surely, then, choose to consume Q_2 units of mineral water, since that level of consumption corresponds to the largest total utility box. Assuming then that the consumer is a "utility maximizer," his *equilibrium* consumption will occur at Q_2 units.

Suppose that the consumer must give up some other desirable good in order to buy mineral water. The position of the utility function in Figure 3.1 may then be thought of as being dependent on the price that the consumer must pay. That is, if a price—higher than the one assumed to exist when line P_1 in Figure 3.1 was drawn—prevailed, the consumer would presumably receive less satisfaction from the consumption of any given quantity of mineral water, since he would have to give up more of the other good in order to pay the higher price. Such a situation is shown by the sloping line P_2. As shown by P_2, the entire utility function would be *shifted* by the higher price (intervening variable).

Given that the consumer is a utility maximizer, and given that there is a second desired good competing for the consumer's dollars, there would be a specific equilibrium level of consumption by the consumer for each possible price level. There would, thus, be a *derived function* relating price to consumption such as that shown in Figure 3.2.

Figure 3.2 is important for two reasons. First, the *idea that an institution responds to changes in the*

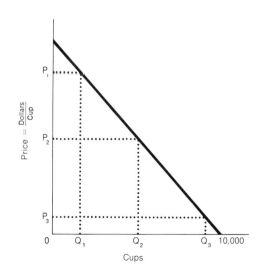

*Figure 3.2
A Demand
Curve*

values of intervening variables by adjusting the equilibrium use of its instruments is the most important idea in this book. It is the touchstone of economic model building. By using this idea, the "ultimate" question of how an institution got where it is can be avoided. By analysis, the amount that a consumer is willing to buy at a given point in time is expected to differ only in response to a specific intervening variable included in the model. Utility, satisfaction, or some other factor got lost in the shuffle. It served just long enough to embody the notion that the consumer reaches a equilibrium level of satisfaction after the consumption of a finite number of units of mineral water.

Second, the function depicted in Figure 3.2 is verifiable empirically. That is, statistical evidence can be collected in order to determine that consumers do, in fact, behave as the hypothesis suggests.

In the following section it will be seen that this hypothesis may be combined with similar hypotheses about the king and the producer in order to discuss the equilibrium of the entire market for mineral water.

THE DEVELOPMENT OF HYPOTHESES

The purpose of this section is to continue the analysis above, focusing this time on the behavior of the king and the mineral-water producer. Our efforts will make it possible to construct a hypothesis that, when tested, will indicate the validity or lack of validity of the entire set of assumptions utilized to describe the market.

Given the behavior of the subject as depicted in Figure 3.2, the explorer-producer may either set a price, say P_2, and see how much mineral water he is able to sell, or produce a specified amount, say Q_3, and see what

price the subject was willing to pay. The total dollars
collected from his sales (revenue) will depend upon both
the price at which the units sell and the number of units
sold. The experience of economists indicates that he will
choose to produce the number of cups designed to return
to him the largest revenue. Put another way, *profits* are
the difference between revenues and costs. Assuming
that the producer does not incur costs in the sale of
mineral water, revenues are equivalent to profits and the
explorer-producer will *act as if* he is a profit maximizer.
Assume, then, that his instrument is the adjustment of the
number of cups that he sells and that his goal is the
maximization of his profits. The explorer-producer must then
choose between alternative output levels. His equilibrium
output will then be associated with the largest profit possible.

The Demand Curve

The essential characteristics of the entire situation are
captured by Figure 3.2. The behavior of the consumer is
represented in that graph as the relationship between
the prices at which cups of water sell and the number of
cups that will be sold. The price at which cups are sold
was measured on the vertical axis of the graph and the
number of cups sold on the horizontal. The line sloping
downward and to the right states that the relationship
between the two variables is one in which the number of
cups sold increases with a decline in the price at which
those cups are sold. In the lingo of economics, that sloping
line is called a *demand curve*. To each price such as P_1
there is a corresponding number of units sold (Q_1). Note
that the price at which the cups sell multiplied by the
number of cups sold is the total revenue from the sale of
the cups. Since the area of a rectangle is the product of

two adjacent sides, the total revenue is found in Figure 3.2
in exactly the same fashion as the total utility was found
in Figure 3.1.

The area of those rectangles would be of considerable
interest to the producer. He would note that the area of
the rectangles related to small levels of unit sales are small,
but he would further note that the areas associated with
large unit sales are also small. Indeed, if he sells as many
as 10,000 cups, he will receive no revenues at all. If he is
to be a profit maximizer, he must find the largest rectangle
capable of fitting into the triangle formed by the demand
curve and the two axes. Alternatively, if he were to plot
the total revenue against the number of units sold on a
second graph, he would find that the relationship looks
like the one depicted in Figure 3.3. Thus, again, his
revenues would reach a maximum with sales of about
5000 units. It may, therefore, be concluded that the
equilibrium output level for the profit-maximizing producer

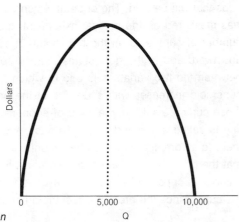

Figure 3.3
A Total
Revenue Function

would in this case be at 5000 units, so long as the king did not interfere.

However, the explorer-producer must reckon with the king who, it will be remembered, is seeking to recover the funds spent to support the explorer on his quest. The explorer must therefore take into account the tax that the king is likely to levy. In graphic terms, the king's intervention may be shown as resulting in a second demand curve lying everywhere below the old demand curve by the amount of the tax. Such a curve appears in Figure 3.4.

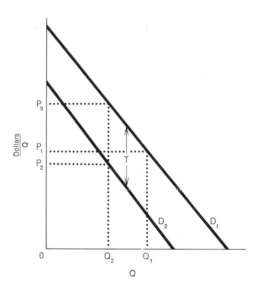

Figure 3.4
A Net
Demand Curve

In effect, the consumer's behavior and the prices that he is willing to pay are still represented by the old demand curve, but the producer now faces a demand curve that is *net* of the tax. That is, while the consumer pays the

price specified by the old demand curve, the producer
receives for himself only that part of the price which is
determined by the new lower demand curve since that
portion of the price which must be paid to the king is
represented by the distance between the two demand
curves. While facing the old demand curve, the producer
would have maximized profits by producing at Q_1. Under
the new situation his profits must be calculated in terms
of the demand curve that is net of the tax. Under such
circumstances it is clear that he would be better off to
select the new profit-maximizing output around Q_2, receive
a net revenue per unit of P_2, and charge his customer a
price P_3. As the level of the unit tax varied from zero
upward, a whole family of *net* demand curves would be
generated. Further, the output calculated to maximize
profit with respect to each new demand curve could be
seen to decline as the size of the tax increases. It must be
concluded, then, that the mineral-water producer will
respond to increases in the level of the tax by reducing his
output and that these output reductions will be
accompanied by rising prices.

Again a testable hypothesis about the response of an
institution has been reached. This time the hypothesis holds
only if all three institutions behave as it has been
supposed they will. That is, the hypothesis will hold only
if the seller, whose behavior has been modeled, acts as if
he has a goal of profit maximization and the king's subject
does not decide to discontinue his search for good health
vis-à-vis the consumption of mineral water. A test of the
hypothesis would test the validity of these assumptions.
Unfortunately, the graphs used up to this point are clumsy
and limited to three-dimensional hypotheses.

For later purposes it will be much more convenient
and tidy to be able to express the relationship between
the output of the producer and the level of the king's tax

in a way that directly specifies both the expected direction
and the expected magnitude of the effect of the one on
the other. In order to do that, it will be necessary for the
reader to develop familiarity with some simple additional
concepts. The results yielded by the algebraic formulation
developed in the next section will be identical to the
above treatment, but will allow the more precise and
flexible specification of functional notation to be used.

AVERAGES, TOTALS, AND MARGINALS

The next several pages will be concerned with exploring the
algebra that deals with inverted U-shaped functions such
as the one illustrated in Figure 3.3. This U-shaped function
nicely expresses what has been discussed and it is a
function that—in one guise or another—appears in many
places in economics.

The function $R = bQ - cQ^2$, when plotted, is shaped
just like the "ant-hill" depicted in Figure 3.5. In that
function, Q stands for the quantity sold to the consumer
and R stands for the total revenue received by the
explorer-producer. The terms b and c are simple constants
replacable by a pair of numbers. While Figure 3.5 contains
a graph of the "ant hill" revenue function, Figure 3.6
graphs the corresponding average and marginal revenue
functions. The reader will note that the *average revenue
function* is nothing more than the demand curve relating
price to output that has been used all along. It is obtained
by dividing total revenue by Q. Thus, $R/Q = b - cQ$.

The Marginal Revenue Function

The *marginal revenue function* is another concept.
The marginal revenue corresponding to any particular
output is defined as the increment to total revenue received

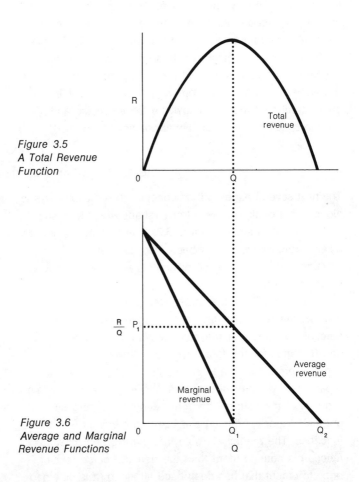

Figure 3.5
A Total Revenue
Function

Figure 3.6
Average and Marginal
Revenue Functions

from the sale of that particular unit. There is *always* a
reason to be interested in the behavior of the marginal
function. In the present case, the marginal function is zero
when the total revenue function is at a *maximum*. Thus,
when faced with a function such as $R = bQ - cQ^2$, it would
not be necessary to plot the function in order to find its

maximum. One need only find the associated marginal revenue function, set it equal to zero, and solve for the value of the output when revenue is maximized. For many explicit total functions of the form in which we are interested, it is possible to directly derive the marginal function by the application of the term nQ^{n-1} to each element of $f(Q)$ where n is the value of the power to which Q is raised. For example, where the total function is expressed as $R = 2Q - 3Q^2$, the associated marginal revenue function is expressed as $dR/dQ = 2 - 6Q$, where dR/dQ is read as the change in revenue associated with a one-unit change in output. The expression dR/dQ is known as the derivative of R with respect to Q.

Since the marginal function can be derived easily from the total function, and the marginal function is equal to zero where the total function reaches its peak, it is easy to find the quantity sold where revenue is maximized. For more complicated functional relationships between variables, other techniques are required, and some are available to insure that the maximum of a particular function has been determined.

The reader will find that it is always important in economic analysis to be able to find the maximum of a particular relationship between inputs and outputs. The general idea is transferable to a wide range of situations and constitutes one of the most important areas in which mathematics is useful to economists.

The Algebra of Curves

The algebra of total, average, and marginal curves may now be used to express the equilibrium model of the mineral-water market. The problem is simply to find an expression of the explorer-producer's revenue-maximizing output that includes the tax levied by the king. That is, he must find an expression for Q as a function of T. But it is now known that maximum output will occur where marginal output is equal to zero. Suppose that the tax levied by the king is T dollars per unit of Q. Equation 3.4 might serve to express the total revenue function.

$$R = 1000Q - .10Q^2 - TQ \qquad (3.4)$$

Taking the derivative of Equation 3.4 and setting the result equal to zero, it is found that

$$\frac{dR}{dQ} = 1000 - .20Q - T = 0 \qquad (3.5)$$

or

$$Q = 5000 - 5T \qquad (3.6)$$

Equation 3.6 indicates that in the absence of a tax the revenue-maximizing number of units sold by the producer will be 5000 (if $T = 0$, $Q = 5000$). For each unit increase in the tax levied by the king, the number of units produced by the explorer will decline by 5 units.

It is not necessary to deal with strictly numerical examples. Beginning with the more general average revenue function provided by Equation 3.7, it is possible to derive the more general relationship between output and the tax rate as follows:

$$P = a - bQ \qquad (3.7)$$

$$R = aQ - bQ^2 \qquad (3.8)$$

$$R = aQ - bQ^2 - TQ \qquad (3.9)$$

$$\frac{dR}{dQ} = a - 2bQ - T = 0 \qquad (3.10)$$

$$Q = \frac{a}{2b} - \frac{T}{2b} \qquad (3.11)$$

If confirmed, hypotheses of the type embodied in

Equation 3.11 can provide the basis for the determination
of optimal "policies" for working with the institutions
involved. For example, Equation 3.11 asserts that an
increase in the tax levied by the king will effect the
level of the output of the mineral-water producer. It further
establishes that the output will decline rather than
increase as a result of an increase in the tax level. An
observant king would note that the heavy-handed increase
in the specific tax on mineral water would finally reduce
the output of the mineral-water producer to zero. He might
also notice that there is some optimal tax designed to
yield the largest revenues for his coffers. To put it another
way, there is a T such that tax revenue (TQ) is at a
maximum.

MODELS AND POLICY MAKING—AN ILLUSTRATION

By making the institutional model encompass hypotheses
about the existence and direction of relationships between
variables, it has been possible to move from a set of
institutional descriptions to a hypothesis capable in
principle, of being confirmed or denied by the observation
of the behavior of the institutions involved. So it is that
model building begins. The process continues as additional
facets of the institutional description and the algebraic
scenario called a *model* are gradually enriched and
explored. The scope of the model usually broadens as
other policy questions begin to occur to the analyst. As
the assumptions underlying the basic model are explored
further, the richness of the method becomes even more
apparent and its great flexibility becomes clear. To illustrate
this proposition and to lay the groundwork for the
discussion of hypothesis testing, the remainder of this

section will be devoted to looking at two further extensions
of the basic mineral-water model.

The Effect of Competition

First, the model will be examined to consider the
implications of the entry of competitors into the producer's
market. This examination will make it apparent that
economic warfare is seldom, if ever, in the best interests
of rational producers. Indeed, producers operating in their
own self-interest will go to considerable lengths to avoid
warfare of the sort to be defined shortly. Where examples
of warfare are thought to exist, it may often be that
more subtle forces are at work.

Second, the model will be enriched to include a
consideration of the role of costs of production in the
determination of the firm's level of output. It will be seen
that different cost structures for the firm will yield quite
different policy conclusions. The work with the second of
these questions will provide a basis for dealing with some
aspects of the economics of higher education in the
following chapter.

Once again the mineral-water producer provides the
narrative with a point of departure. On p. 44 it was observed
that the producer treated the demand curve for his
product as a fixed statement about the behavior of the
consumer. Assuming a fixed demand curve, the only
responses available to the producer are the adjustment of
price or output. If thus followed from the earlier discussion
that the single level of price consistent with profit
maximization is the level of P_1 in Figure 3.6, where the
marginal revenue of the producer is equal to zero. The
entry of additional producers into the market would not in
in any way change the position of the demand curve.
As was observed earlier, the demand curve is a statement

about the behavior of consumers. It is a statement about
their tastes and responses to price changes. Except in
certain odd cases, the arrival of a second mineral-water
producer with an identical product should not have any
influence on the consumer's behavior as reflected in the
demand curve.

The arrival of a second producer of mineral water would
present something of a problem to a previously happy and
contented monopolist. The addition of any further
quantities of mineral water to the market would simply
serve to reduce the total revenue just as it would if the
explorer-producer had full control of the market as he did
in the original scenario.

At first glance, it might seem to be in the original
producer's best interest to increase production to Q_2, driving
the price to zero and his new competitor out of business.
An even more violent solution would be to pay a buyer
of the mineral water to haul it away and suffer the losses
incurred thereby until the competitor gave in. Both of
these strategies commit the producer to a period of
indefinite lost profits or outlays, which would end only
when one of the producers ran out of resources. A true
profit maximizer would observe that he would be better
advised to negotiate. The original explorer-producer can
afford to pay up to a fraction of a cent less than his total
expected profits in order to keep a second producer out of
production. The newcomer is, of course, in an identical
position. The conclusion to the first policy question is
thus that some form of market-sharing arrangement or
payoff is superior to price warfare from the point of view
of both parties.

Two largely independent outcomes are possible as the
number of rivals increases beyond two (the *duopoly case*).
If the number of rivals is few (the *oligopoly case*),
agreements may be reached to allow the genteel sharing

of profits. Thus, in all likelihood, the level of production in the market would remain at Q_1. In the admittedly unlikely event that a large number of producers were able to reach an agreement, the profits would be divided between so many firms that the profit share of the individual firm might fall close to zero. That outcome is a special case of what is called *monopolistic competition.* The availability of profits would seem likely to lure new firms into the market. If the number of firms were very large, it is most likely that firms would be attracted until output reached Q_2. In that pure competition case, price and revenue in the market would fall to zero.

The oversimplified discussion of the last paragraph contains the central idea on which the social regulation of monopoly is based. From the consumer's point of view, the monopoly outcome differs considerably from the competitive outcome. In the monopoly case the consumer is asked to pay a relatively high price for a good that is made available by the monopolist or by a collusive group. Furthermore, the amount of the good that is made available to consumers is considerably less than the amount that would be available if agreement among a large number of competitors was impossible.

Without modifying the model, then, further analysis leads to the conclusion that there are strong incentives working in favor of producer collusion. Further, the resource dollars spent on goods produced under collusive conditions exceed those necessary to sustain the production of the goods if produced by a large number of small producers.

To the extent that it is anticipated that producers will incur costs of production, the conclusions reached may be modified considerably. Turn now to a consideration of how costs might be included in the simple mineral-water model.

Producer Equilibrium with Costs

Suppose that the explorer-producer decides to retire from
actively running his own stand and to hire a young lady
to serve the mineral spring water to his customer. Suppose
further that he agrees to (a) pay her a commission on
each cup sold, (b) pump the water from the spring to a
roadside stand with a pump requiring electricity in amounts
that rise as the square of the volume of water pumped,
and (c) build the stand. Assuming that electricity is available
at some constant price, the total costs for the operation
of the roadside stand (C) may be expressed as follows:

$$C = dQ^2 + eQ + F \qquad\qquad (3.12)$$

where d is the unit cost of electricity to pump the water
from the spring, e is the commission to be paid to the
young lady, and F is the one-time cost of purchasing
the pump and erecting the stand.

There are two conceptually distinct cost elements each
of which must be kept in mind. First, there are costs
resulting from the particular choice of the technology of
production and, second, there are costs associated with
the payments to the *factors of production* such as the
electricity and the young lady.

As the expression is constructed, the term Q^2 illustrates
a technological matter with which the producer must cope.
If, in fact, other ways were discovered in which water could
be pumped to the stand, that term in the expression would
have to be changed. It would also have to be changed
if the price of electricity (d) varied according to the
quantity used by the producer. As it stands, the technology
of water pumping drives the average cost upward as the
producer's output increases. The producer experiences
rising costs simply as a reflection of the underlying
technology. Such rising costs due to technological factors

are termed *technological diseconomies of scale.* If the young lady insisted that her commission *rate* increase with each additional cup sold, the producer would be said to experience *pecuniary diseconomies* of scale. However, if costs fell rather than rose in these two cases, the producer would be said to face technological and pecuniary *economies of scale.*

It may be noted in passing that the presence or absence of economies, whatever their source, may sometimes be the key to the number of entrants likely to be attracted to a particular market. If diseconomies cause a rapid rise in the costs of firms that are very small relative to the total size of the market, the market will probably be populated by a very large number of small firms. If, however, economies of scale persist through a range of firm sizes approaching the size of the total market, a *natural monopoly* is said to exist. The agricultural industries.of the United States are characterized by the former, while the railroads are considered an example of the latter.

In order to see in precisely what fashion the profit-maximizing firm is affected by economies and diseconomies of scale, it is useful to first examine how easily the earlier analysis may be altered to include costs in the maximization scheme of the mineral spring operator. In the absence of costs the profits of the producer were treated as equal to the revenues from the sale of the mineral spring water. Thus,

$$R = aQ - bQ^2 \tag{3.13}$$

was differentiated, set equal to zero, and solved for the value of output at which profits were maximized. If profits are defined as the difference between costs and revenues, an almost identical expression results if Equation 3.12 is subtracted from Equation 3.13. Thus,

$$\text{Total profit} = R - C \tag{3.14}$$

$$= (aQ - bQ^2) - (dQ^2 + eQ + F) \tag{3.15}$$

combining terms we have

$$\text{Total profit} = -(b + d)Q^2 + (a - e)Q + F \tag{3.16}$$

As the reader will recognize, Equation 3.16 is of precisely the same form as the total revenue equation alone, with the added term F. The shape of the total profit curve is thus roughly the same as the shape of the total revenue curve, and the maximum point of the total profit curve may be found in the same way that the maximum point of the total revenue curve was found. Thus, Equation 3.16 is differentiated, set equal to zero, and solved for the profit-maximizing output.

$$\frac{d \text{ profit}}{dQ} = -2(b + d)Q + e = 0 \tag{3.17}$$

$$Q = \frac{a - e}{2(b + d)} \tag{3.18}$$

The result in Equation 3.18 may be arrived at in a slightly different but highly enlightening way. By rearranging it, we may see that Equation 3.18 has an interesting interpretation. Just as the equations for total revenue and for total profit possessed related marginal and average functions, so does the equation for total cost.

$$\text{Average cost} = dQ + e + \frac{Q}{F} \tag{3.19}$$

$$\text{Marginal cost} = 2dQ + e \tag{3.20}$$

But Equation 3.18, rearranged slightly, will show

$$a - 2bQ = 2dQ + e \tag{3.21}$$

The right-hand side of Equation 3.21 is the expression for marginal cost and the left-hand side is the familiar expression for marginal revenue. Thus, it may be concluded, on the basis of Equation 3.19, that the producer should continue to adjust production until the addition to revenue from the sale of the last unit (marginal revenue) is just equal to the increment to cost incurred from the production of the last unit (marginal cost). Just as equating marginal revenue to zero in the case of the costless producer yielded a maximum profit, equating marginal revenue to marginal cost determines a profit maximum in the presence of costs. Figure 3.7 illustrates the resulting equilibrium graphically.

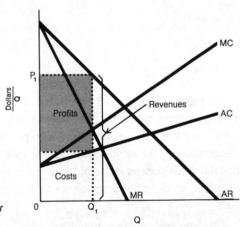

Figure 3.7
Equilibrium of
the Mineral-Water
Producer

The demand and marginal revenue curves of Figure 3.7 relate to the earlier total revenue equation. The marginal cost curve and average cost curve relate to Equations 3.19 and 3.20. The marginal cost curve intersects the marginal revenue curve at Q_1. The price that the consumer is willing to pay is P_1. The producer's profit appears as the shaded box. The vertical distance from the average cost curve to the average revenue curve determines the average profit.

The reader may note that the cost curve in Figure 3.7 is depicted as sloping upward and to the right. A firm operating under such cost conditions is said to be subject to *diseconomies of scale.* If, as in Figure 3.8, the average

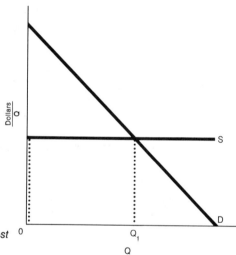

Figure 3.8
The Constant-Cost Producer

(and marginal) cost curve is horizontal, the firm is said to face *constant costs.* The firm depicted in Figure 3.9, whose cost curves slope downward and to the right, is said to be subject to *economies of scale.*

Taxation

The earlier discussion of taxation and the mineral-water producer focused on the responses of the mineral-water

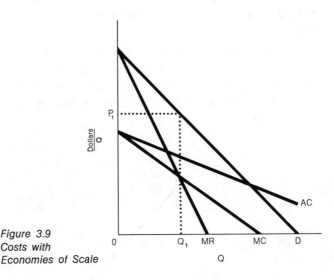

Figure 3.9
Costs with
Economies of Scale

producer to changes in the tax rates levied by the king.
Given the discussion of the present section, it can be
shown that the introduction of cost considerations will
modify the responses of the producer and, depending
on the case and the policy maker's point of view, result
in more or less desirable outcomes. These results can be
discerned when the single-firm monopolist is examined
under conditions of constant, increasing, and decreasing
costs.

In the case of constant costs, the equilibrium output
of this monopolistic producer will be smaller than that of
his zero-cost counterpart, as is illustrated in Figure 3.10.
In that figure the output of the zero-cost producer would
be Q_2, while the output of the positive-cost producer would
be at Q_1. In the presence of a tax in the amount T, the
monopolistic producer would reduce his output to the
new equilibrium at Q_3 and the consumer would be forced

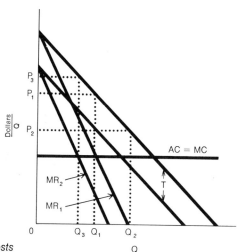

Figure 3.10
Equilibrium of
the Monopolist.
with Constant Costs

to pay the higher price P_3. It may be observed that in this
case the price rises by less than the full amount of the
tax. In other words, the burden of the tax falls partly
upon the consumer who now pays a price increased over
the pretax price by just the amount of the tax and partly
upon the producer who receives lower revenues. It will be
seen that the burden falls somewhat differently in the
other two cases to be discussed.

In the case of the increasing-cost firm, the tax similarly
reduces the output of the firm from Q_2 to Q_1, as is
illustrated in Figure 3.11. However, in this second case
the burden of the tax again does not fall wholly on the
consumer, but is divided between the consumer and the
producer. It does fall somewhat more heavily on
the producer since the price *does not* rise by the full
amount of the tax. The reason for this is that the reduction
in the output of the firm is accompanied by a reduction

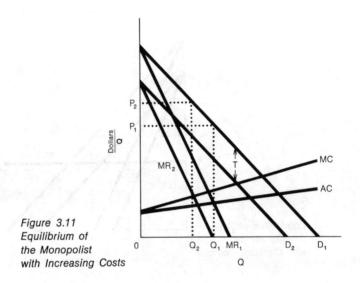

Figure 3.11
Equilibrium of
the Monopolist
with Increasing Costs

in the costs of production. These cost reductions then
serve to partially offset the increased price brought on by
the tax.

As is shown in Figure 3.12, the consumer is not so
fortunate in the case of a tax levied on a decreasing cost-
producer. The price rise faced in that case exceeds the
amount of the tax since the tax-induced reduction in output
causes the producer to operate at somewhat higher
costs than those incurred during the pretax equilibrium.

Finally, consider the case of a tax levied directly on the
profits of each of these producers as opposed to the unit
tax discussed thus far. In each of the pretax equilibriums
it has been noted that there is no alternative level of
output that will yield higher levels of profits for the producer.
Thus, a tax that was levied directly on that profit should
not be expected to produce a change in the equilibrium
output of the producer. The policy implications of a tax

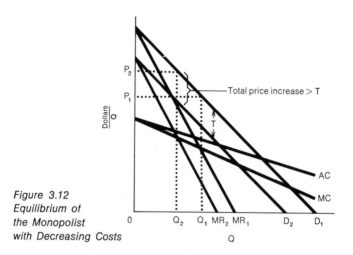

Figure 3.12
Equilibrium of
the Monopolist
with Decreasing Costs

on profits are therefore quite different from those of a
tax on unit sales. In the event that a unit tax is levied, the
producer can be expected always to reduce output.
The result, invariably, is an increased price. When a profits
tax is levied, no alternative output capable of bringing
greater profits to the producer exists; he is therefore forced
to stay where he is and bear the full burden of the
tax.

   The results of the analysis hopefully illustrate that a
wise king or government will study carefully the industry
under consideration for increased taxes in order to
anticipate the consequences of alternative tax policies.
In such an analysis a king might note that (a) the burden
of the tax is dependent on the cost structure of the firms
in the industry, (b) the firms will respond differently
to different taxes, and (c) the tax may, in effect, promote
either increased efficiency in cost terms or, in some
cases, increased inefficiency in cost terms. These

are considerations that must be taken into account if the
final outcomes of particular taxes are to be understood.

THINKING WITH CHAPTER 3

Chapter 3 has engaged in an altogether too sober
look at the development of a set of institutional models
from the starting institutional descriptions. It has touched
lightly, perhaps too lightly, on the responses of a firm under
various conditions (in the face of different relations among
intervening variables) that might reasonably be expected
to define the environment in which it operates.

The particular topics covered in connection with the
firm are not nearly as important as the use to which the
concepts of function and equilibrium were put. Those
concepts and the tools for their expression in the context
of a model have, and will continue to have, much broader
applications than have been demonstrated here. The
importance of these applications is not so much in the
"realism" or "truth" of the resulting insights as in the
alternative points of view, or ways of solving problems,
that they help to generate.

The reader is now urged to attempt to build simple
models of his own utility-maximizing behavior. Just as it
was necessary to apply the concepts of institutional
description in order to give them meaning, it is necessary
for a reader to construct a number of simple models in
order to get a feel for that portion of the process of
economic thought. The reader will soon find that it is
possible to construct simple models rapidly, and that these
models may be used to explore the implications of decision
making in particular areas.

The reader may find it helpful to consider the institutional
descriptions used by other students who set about the
construction of their own models as a means of beginning

the analysis of models. Think for a moment about the
notion that smoking is an instrument for utility maximization.
It is often true that the reader increases his consumption
of cigarettes as a function of the time remaining until
some particular kinds of actions must be taken. If hours
of study are an instrument for grade-point maximization,
what are the effects of various intervening variables on
the number of hours during which the reader studies.
One student constructed a model to test the hypothesis
that her little sister tormented the family cat as a
function of the amount of attention paid to her by the
grown-ups in her family. What is the appropriate formulation
of a model leading to that hypothesis? What factors
(intervening variables) influence the number of social
outings that the reader undertakes in a given time period?
How might a model illustrating those factors and their
relationship to dating be constructed? What attributes of
a given situation govern the number of miles traveled
by automobile on a given date?

The reader is urged to use his imagination in constructing
models and developing a facility for their use. In the
following chapter a simple model of university behavior
will be constructed in connection with exploring the testing
of hypotheses. Hopefully, that model will illustrate
something of the spirit in which such models should
be constructed.

4

statistical
description

To the questions of institutional description and "So what?" must be added the question "What is the evidence to support your hypothesis?" The latter question should usually be asked with considerably greater care than the preceding ones. It presumes that the reader is satisfied with the institutional descriptions and model presented and has agreed that the hypothesis is testable. Usually, a discussion should not proceed up to the evidence. To ask prematurely for evidence is to court disaster. As Sky Masterson's daddy was reported to have said, "Son, if the man says that he'll bet you he can make the deuce of spades leap out of your ear and spit in your eye, don't take that bet." Seldom do good hypotheses want for lack of data to test them. Even less often do suspicious hypotheses want for data since they have usually been derived from the data which the analyst would like to use in testing the hypothesis. Often they have been derived by the techniques to be discussed in this chapter. In short, much of the effort in the social sciences, and all of the effort of the preceding two chapters, is aimed at avoiding the misleading conclusions that "experience" leads to.

Chapters 2 and 3 developed a means for describing the behavior of institutions and translating those descriptions into testable hypotheses. The present chapter will develop some ideas that are useful in the testing of such hypotheses.

It is useful to continue with the notion of the economist as a black box. The testing procedure may then be characterized as involving (a) a new set of inputs to the black box and (b) a second process going on inside the black box. The new set of inputs is a second description of the behavior of the institution under study. The second process is that of comparing the new description with the hypothesis developed in the modeling effort.

The goal of the testing procedure is to develop a

description of the relationship between two variables
—that is, to determine whether such a relationship
exists, and if it does, its direction, magnitude, and
agreement or conflict with the hypothesis that led to the
test. Three questions are thus involved: (a) Is there a
relationship between a particularly interesting pair of
variables? (b) If the relationship exists, in what new
direction will an increase or decrease in one induce the
others to go? (c) What will be the magnitude of that
induced change? We have demonstrated that a
hypothesis provides a set of qualitative assertions as to
what the answers to those questions will be in a particular
case.

The new inputs to the process discussed above are
descriptions of the individual variables involved. The
process is that of describing the relationship between
the two variables in such a way that the description is
comparable to the hypotheses developed as in the previous
chapter. First, consider some of the ideas used in describing
individual variables.

THE DESCRIPTION OF INDIVIDUAL VARIABLES

In an almost unconscious manner most of us seek and
use statistical information in the solution of our problems.
An individual who is about to take an auto trip will usually
collect various kinds of information on which to base his
preparations for that trip. What distance is to be driven?
How long will it take to make the drive? In what condition
are the roads? Where are the good restaurants? Similarly,
in deciding whether or not to take a blind date, a student
will ask a range of questions on which the decision or
decisions will be based.

Based on experience, the individual assumes that a set
of relationships among a certain kind of "variables"

exists, and he therefore makes a set of policies to govern
his decisions or, if necessary, makes the set of decisions
required. Thus, the selection of a "best route" at the
beginning of a trip is a "policy selection" which would be
subject to modification on the basis of the events encountered while actually carrying out the trip.

In the same casual spirit many readers undoubtedly
engaged in the limited statistical consideration of colleges
and universities before deciding where to enroll. The
"grapevine" or a *Playboy* "survey" may have helped in
determining the value of some important variables. Those
matters aside, the admissions officer of one highly
competitive institution behaves as if there are three
variables of great importance to students choosing an
institution of higher learning (IHL). These variables are
the enrollment of the institution, the cost of tuition, room,
and board, and the quality of the competition to be
expected by the student.

Experience with universities is by no means acquired
as easily as experience with long trips. Therefore, at simple
levels, some of the tools of simple statistical description
might have been helpful in aiding the reader to come
to a decision.

Use of Tables

The *reference table,* which arranges data in columns, is
an important, but not terribly informative housekeeping
device or depository for data. Table 4.1 contains the size,
cost of attendance, and a measure of the competitiveness,
as well as degree production and faculty size, for 97
universities. It will be of interest in the present discussion.
In using a reference table, the reader may ask "What does
it tell me at a glance?" The smallest observations, the
largest observations, and sometimes trends over time can

be observed without great difficulty. Unfortunately, such
tables yield superficial information at first glance.
It is the further work carried out on the observations
contained in such tables that will give worthwhile insights.
Meanwhile, primary data tables serve as convenient and
reliable repositories. See Table 4.1.

TABLE 4.1

SELECTED CHARACTERISTICS OF 97 MAJOR COLLEGES AND UNIVERSITIES

Out-of-State Tuition (1)	Degrees (2)	Student Enrollment (3)	Faculty (4)	Average Entering SAT (5)
$ 850	3,096	13,136	1,634	4
2,275	291	1,211	192	1
1,104	3,787	23,357	2,025	4
700	2,141	10,748	1,993	4
720	2,777	13,236	1,515	2
1,000	1,699	6,401	—	2
1,850	4,746	23,011	1,680	2
700	3,824	20,375	—	4
650*	3,723	24,101	1,364	2
2,300	1,184	5,042	914	1
702	2,877	19,113	3,238	2
2,100	396	1,520	3,631	1
1,525	7,455	121,010	—	3
2,100	1,125	5,228	573	1
2,100	2,5/7	10,464	4,141	3
1,215	2,866	27,264	2,482	3
486	4,315	29,263	1,185	3
1,310	2,428	14,565	1,304	4
1,383	3,661	27,560	—	3
2,100	6,704	17,459	3,355	1
705	2,928	16,361	2,122	3
2,350	3,574	19,438	3,756	1
2,350	970	3,929	440	1
1,875	2,004	8,595	691	3
2,000	1,675	7,552	1,262	1
975	4,574	20,915	2,808	2
2,000	2,160	10,450	—	2
1,875	3,419	17,714	—	2
1,068	1,520	8,870	998	1

TABLE 4.1 *(Continued)*

Out-of-State Tuition (1)	Degrees (2)	Student Enrollment (3)	Faculty (4)	Average Entering SAT (5)
765	3,887	20,470	1,947	3
2,000	4,696	20,345	6,451	1
460	3,480	25,555	1,182	3
1,800	988	8,471	629	1
964	9,388	33,124	7,983	2
1,490	7,758	48,563	3,381	3
1,005	2,766	16,925	2,355	2
1,000	4,033	18,659	2,526	3
2,250	1,602	10,036	—	1
798	3,251	15,791	2,538	3
788	2,130	12,596	1,518	3
980	2,599	15,553	1,917	4
2,000	1,237	4,982	568	1
820	3,579	20,247	3,489	4
854	5,645	37,898	3,830	—
2,245	1,994	7,730	—	1
740	2,395	15,202	—	3
1,200	2,455	11,056	1,270	2
1,747	2,645	14,530	1,372	4
1,265	8,485	38,758	4,569	1
1,540	8,882	37,284	6,801	1
951	7,706	58,304	5,908	2
870	7,100	41,855	4,231	4
933	4,545	18,303	—	3
1,635	1,786	9,726	1,031	2
2,275	6,939	34,582	4,092	2
862	1,821	11,317	2,372	2
862	3,497	15,601	1,919	2
475	2,677	15,098	835	4
2,190	3,547	17,239	1,898	2
2,050	2,082	7,723	998	2
2,350	607	2,616	—	1
1,110	7,486	38,834	4,396	4
1,220	3,142	16,187	1,509	3
950	2,898	17,354	2,067	3
900	3,260	18,940	1,083	4
999	2,867	13,314	1,625	4
999	3,521	13,959	1,883	4
1,200	5,626	33,742	5,090	2

TABLE 4.1 *(Continued)*

Out-of-State Tuition (1)	Degrees (2)	Student Enrollment (3)	Faculty (4)	Average Entering SAT (5)
2,150	4,059	19,417	3,862	1
1,500	3,321	22,067	2,502	1
1,900	914	5,338	348	2
2,350	1,287	4,756	1,487	1
1,200	4,780	23,588	4,234	—
468	3,587	23,146	1,210	—
2,435	1,322	5,816	680	1
1,910	555	2,807	414	1
2,300	1,693	8,423	2,902	1
830	4,726	27,174	—	2
1,850	4,637	18,692	331	—
2,145	3,913	11,556	2,514	1
2,260	208	1,024	175	1
2,250	4,004	20,254	—	2
1,410	4,114	33,653	2,301	4
975	3,790	20,832	3,376	4
742	2,321	12,025	1,802	5
509	2,615	18,835	966	4
502	8,098	30,628	2,886	4
2,475	1,324	5,048	1,042	1
843	1,747	19,265	—	5
939	2,835	18,537	1,092	4
825	2,216	11,609	1,422	3
2,100	2,061	11,908	1,636	1
825	5,762	30,357	4,279	2
1,140	5,083	32,370	2,088	4
910	2,503	14,041	1,975	4
1,150	9,174	33,000	5,884	2
2,350	2,224	8,665	—	1

Sources:

Column (1): *New York Times Encyclopedic Almanac, 1970* (New York: The New York Times, 1969).

Column (2): Marjorie O. Chandler and Mary Evans Hooper, *Earned Degrees Conferred: 1967–1968—Part A—Summary Data,* the Office of Education, U.S. Department of Health, Education and Welfare (Washington, D.C.: Government Printing Office, May 1969).

Column (3): Marjorie O. Chandler and Mabel C. Rice, *Opening Fall Enrollment in Higher Education, 1967,* the Office of Education, U.S. Department of Health, Education and Welfare (Washington, D.C.: Government Printing Office, 1967).

Column (4): R. Beazley, *Numbers and Characteristics of Employees in Institutions of Higher Education, Fall 1966* (Washington, D.C.: Government Printing Office, 1969).
Column (5): *New York Times Encyclopedic Almanac, 1970, op. cit.*

The relatively incomprehensible form of Table 4.1 is worth contrasting with the *analytic* form of Table 4.2. In Table 4.2, the IHLs have been classified by the size and SAT score given in Table 4.1. The level of nonresident tuition has been entered in the appropriate cell. Though Table 4.2 contains most of the information contained in Table 4.1, the act of *classification* has made clear in the analytic table a number of characteristics of the observations not evident in Table 4.1. Large IHLs are seen to be more strongly represented than small IHLs. There are relatively few institutions with SAT levels below 475. On the whole, small IHLs with low SAT scores are absent from the particular population displayed in Table 4.2. Finally, there is a tendency for schools where competition as measured by SAT scores is highest to charge high tuitions.

While it is possible to refine each impression gained from the data, the present section is concerned with descriptions of single variables. Consider, then, how just the data about the size of the institutions listed in Table 4.2 may be treated so as to make that data (a) easily understood and (b) easily comparable to similar descriptions of other populations of IHLs.

The impression related about the size of the IHLs has two dimensions of concern to us here. We need to know (a) how large those institutions are and (b) the degree to which they tend to differ from one another. Both of these dimensions (and others not of interest here) are conveyed in the *histogram* of Figure 4.1. The histogram conveys, in visual form, the number of IHLs in each size-category used in Table 4.2. All histograms are constructed

TABLE 4.2

TUITION RATES FOR SELECTED UNIVERSITIES
BY SAT SCORE AND ENROLLMENT[a]

Average Entering SAT Score	Size of Institution				
	1–2500	2500–5000	5000–7000	7500–10,000	10,000–15,000
625+	$ 2275	$ 2350	$ 2100	$ 2000	$ 2145
	2100	2000	1900	1068	2100
	2260	2350	2435	1800	2250
		1910	2475	2300	
		2350	2300	2245	
				2350	
575–625			$ 1000	$ 1635	$ 720
				2050	1200
					862
					2000
525–575				$ 1875	$ 2100
					788
					825
475–525					$ 850
					700
					1310
					1747
					999
					999
					910
475–					$ 742
	3	5	6	9	18

[a] For sources, see Table 4.1.

TABLE 4.2 *(Continued)*

| | | | Number of Insti- |
	15,000– 20,000	20,000– 30,000	30,000+	tutions
$ 2100	$ 2000	$ 1265	
2350	1500	1540	
			28
$ 702	$ 1850	$ 964	
1005	650	951	
1000	975	2275	
862	830	1200	25
2190	2250	825	
2150		1150	
1875			
$ 705	$ 1525	$ 1490	
798	1215		
1220	486		
950	765		17
740	440		
933	1383		
$ 980	$ 1104	$ 870	
475	820	1110	
900	975	1410	
509	700	502	21
939		1140	
$ 843			2
21	17	14	93

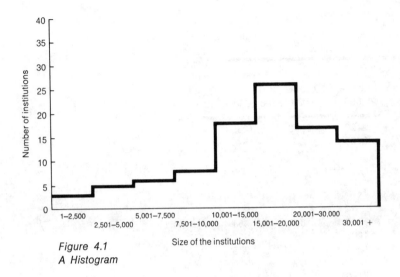

Figure 4.1
A Histogram

according to the same rules governing the construction of
Figure 4.1. That is, the width of each bar is proportional
to the size of the class interval on the horizontal axis and
the height of the bar is proportional to the number of
units contained in the size-class corresponding to the bar.

The impression that the institutions are relatively large
is derived from the fact of the relative heights of the
higher-enrollment categories. It is also clear from the
histogram that there are considerable size-differences
among the IHLs. Once again, these visual impressions are
gained much more quickly in the histogram than from the
relatively clumsy but more precise mediums of Tables
4.1 or 4.2.

The statistical terms *mean* and *standard deviation* are
those words in the language of statistics that place
specific numerical values on the impressions gained from
the histogram.

The *mean,* or arithmetic average, is a *measure of central tendency.* Any measure of central tendency attempts to describe a histogram by the use of a single number. If a population of IHLs is described as being "small," the mean size of that population will reveal some notion as to *how* small. The standard deviation, as will be seen, is a measure of "how seriously" to take that mean. It indicates just how far the individual members of the population are likely to diverge from the mean. Put another way, the standard deviation tells just who in a group is really small and who is extraordinarily large.

The mean is computed by summing the values of the individual observations on the variable and dividing by the number of observations. In functional form:

$$\text{Arithmetic mean} = \bar{X} = \frac{\Sigma X}{N}$$

where $\bar{X}$ stands for the mean, N stands for the number of observations, and Σ is a summation sign to be read "the sum of."

As has been said, the standard deviation summarizes the degree to which the individual observations in a set of observations depart from their mean value. If the mean of a particular set of observations is $\bar{X}$, the distance separating a particular observation X from the mean may obviously be determined by subtracting $\bar{X}$ from X. By summing the *absolute values* of all such distances (the distance without reference to sign) and dividing the total by N, the *average deviation* is obtained.

$$\text{Average deviation} = \frac{\Sigma |X - \bar{X}|}{N}$$

Now, if the average deviation is thought of as an index of the degree to which individual observations depart from the mean, it would not alter that particular meaning if the index were simply squared. The variance is computed by doing just that. The standard deviation is the square root of the variance. It appears in functional form as:

$$\text{Standard deviation} = S_d = \sqrt{\frac{\Sigma(X - \bar{X})^2}{N}}$$

But, under the assumption that the histogram of the total population from which the observations were drawn is roughly bell shaped, the standard deviation has an important advantage over the average deviation as an desirable index. It allows the following interpretations. About 66 percent of all observations can be expected to fall within one standard deviation of the mean and about 95 percent of all observations will lie within two standard deviations of the mean.

Two important features of Figure 4.1 may thus be conveyed by stating that the mean and standard deviation are 16,922 enrollees and 17,870 enrollees, respectively. These numbers suggest to the practiced analyst that enrollments between 0 and about 34,000 are quite common, but that fewer than 1 IHL in 20 exceeds 53,000 enrollees.

It is also a matter of interest that the statistical word $\Sigma(X - \bar{X})^2$ is a direct measure of the *total variation* in the size of these IHLs. If one variable is purported to influence another variable, the variation in the one should, by some measure, be related to the variation in the other. The total variation will thus be of direct interest when the relationship between the two variables is considered.

So a simple statistical description leaves the reader with a means of constructing concise and revealing descriptions of observations on particular variables. In addition, the ideas will prove to be important in working with the relationship between variables.

Before moving to discuss relationships between variables, let us note that the concepts to be discussed can be used alone or in conjunction with the model-building techniques of the previous chapter. Used alone, the concepts can produce all manner of illusory beliefs about the causal arrangements between variables. Only if the user is willing to *think* with and apply the concepts of model building can he have some assurance that reliable predictions will be forthcoming. Consider, therefore, before proceeding, a model of IHL behavior based on the mineral-water producer model of the previous chapter.

The following question may well have occurred to the reader by now: "If colleges and universities are decision makers, in what ways may their decision making influence the final outcomes for students?" It is possible to treat only a small portion of the problem here, but in doing so the complimentary nature of model building and statistical analysis may come somewhat clearer. The reader may also find a modest element of fun in considering the caricature of the IHL presented.

Consider the idea of a profit-maximizing university. Consider such a university facing a population of students (consumers) maximizing utility through paying tuition so as to get a degree. The wise, beneficient university, of course, would adjust degree output so as to maximize profits (a tale with a familiar ring).

A small kernel may be chosen from Chapter 3 for further examination, namely, costs. Are costs decreasing in such a way that the IHLs will grow large enough to produce a continuing supply of degrees at lower and lower unit costs? Are costs increasing? Do costs limit optimal institutions to a small and cloister-like scale so that a rising demand must bring forth new institutions or, under some circumstances, dilute the quality of the old?

RELATIONSHIPS BETWEEN VARIABLES

Testing the Model; the Scatter Diagram

As a first step in examining the plausibility of the model, assume that each state in the United States is a different

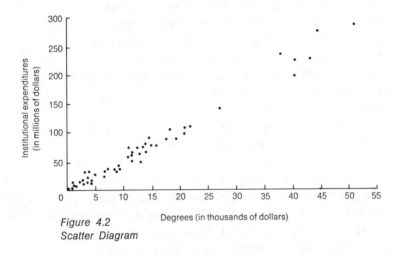

Figure 4.2
Scatter Diagram

"firm" in the "degree market" and examine the relationship
between instructional expenditures and degree production
in the states. A basic statistical device, the *scatter
diagram,* is used in Figure 4.2 to display instructional
expenditures and degrees granted, by state. All scatter
diagrams are constructed with reference to the rules used
to construct Figure 4.2. That is, for each unit under study
(in this case, each state) a point is marked whose X axis
coordinate denotes the value of one characteristic of the
unit and whose Y axis coordinate denotes the value of a
second, supposedly related characteristic of the unit. The
expenditures in 1963 are assumed to have influenced
the number of degrees granted in 1967. To the extent
that the points plotted fall along a line, the device suggests
that there is some relationship between the two variables.
Figure 4.2 tends to confirm the existence of a strong
positive association between expenditures made and
degrees produced by the states. Figure 4.3 illustrates
several alternative results which plotting these figures

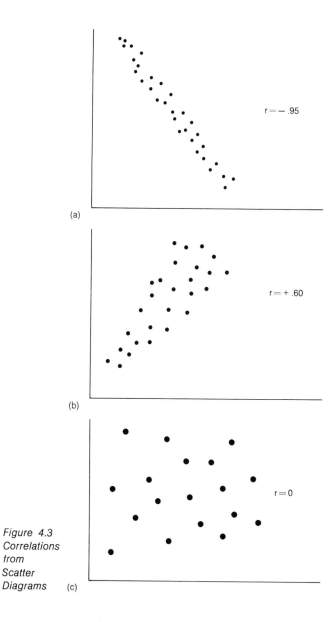

r = − .95

(a)

r = + .60

(b)

r = 0

Figure 4.3
Correlations
from
Scatter
Diagrams   (c)

might have produced. Figure 4.3(a) shows the result that would confirm a strong negative relationship. Figure 4.3(b) is suggestive of a much weaker positive relationship, and Figure 4.3(c) suggests that no simple and apparent relationship exists between the two variables being considered.

It may not be said, on the basis of any of these figures, that one variable "causes" another. At most it can be said that the evidence does not deny causality. Causal contentions are properties of the models of Chapter 3.

The *correlation coefficient (r)* is a statistical term capable of succinctly describing the visual relationship conveyed by the scatter diagram in much the same way that the mean conveys an idea about a histogram. It ranges in value from -1.0 to $+1.0$; these values describe perfect negative and positive linear relationships, respectively. A feel for the range of these relationships may be gotten by considering the values of r found in Figure 4.3.

Figures 4.4(a), (b), and (c) illustrate the *total* cost curves related to increasing-, decreasing-, and constant-cost industries respectively. Suppose, now, that the pattern of degree production and expenditures on higher education by the state are paralleled in the major universities in each state. That is, assume that degree production and expenditures in each state are controlled by one institution. A comparison of the curves in Figure 4.4 with the pattern of the plots in Figure 4.2 tends to suggest that the increasing cost relationship of Figure 4.4(a) may relate most closely with that shown in Figure 4.2, though it is possible that constant costs are present.

It may be recalled from Chapter 3 that total costs may be influenced by either technological or pecuniary considerations. Thus, either rising factor costs or decreasing factor returns might be responsible for diseconomies of scale. *Decreasing returns,* in this context, means that each

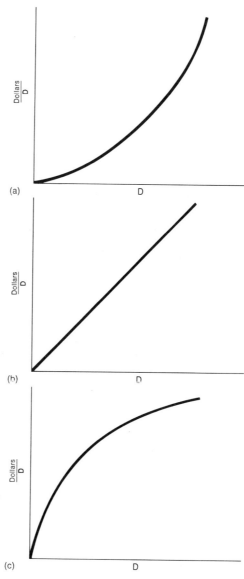

(a)

D

(h)

D

(c)

D

*Figure 4.4
Scatter Diagram:
Degree
Production and
Expenditures
on Higher
Education*

additional input yields a smaller increment to total output
than did its predecessor.

It is, in fact, convenient to think, for a moment, of
universities as black boxes into which factors of production
are put and from which degree holders pour forth after a
time lapse. If universities controlled only their degree
requirements and all students were full-time students, it
might be judged that the average time required to receive
a degree is four years. Thus the number of degrees
produced would, in a given year, be about one fourth of
the enrollees. In functional form,

$$D = a + bE$$

where D is the number of degrees, E is the number of
students enrolled in a given year, $a = 0$ and $b = .25$.

The "naive" model of the above paragraph may be
"tested" by plotting the number of degrees produced in a
given year against the enrollments for that year. The results
of such a plot for the 97 universities considered earlier
appears in Figure 4.5. As seen through that diagram, the
hypothesis does not fare too badly. Given the scales on
the two axes, the line $D = 0 + .25E$ should pass though
the origin and the two points should be marked with
x's (i.e., the line has a slope 5:20). Instead, it can be
noted, a line trying to pass through the dense clusters of
points is somewhat flatter (i.e., the straight line has a
slope close to 4:25). From this result, it can be concluded
that universities graduate only about one student for
each six enrolled. Furthermore, it may be seen that the
relationship grows less reliable as the institution size
increases. That is, the observations "fan out" from the
line as one moves northeast from the origin.

The use of scatter diagrams is clearly an important and
simple way to obtain first impressions about relationships
between variables. Indeed, in the statistical analysis of

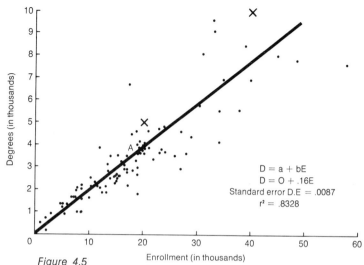

Figure 4.5
Scatter Diagram: Degrees Produced and Total Enrollment
for 97 Universities

such relationships this step should not be skipped, since
it will often reveal important features of a relationship that
are not revealed by the direct numerical techniques. For
example, the techniques to be discussed below would not
reveal the apparent curvature visible in Figure 4.2, nor
would they reveal the tendency for the observations in
Figure 4.5 to "fan out" as the institution size increases. It is,
however, both important and convenient for the sake of
efficiency and accuracy of estimation to translate the
scatter diagram into the algebraic language of the
equilibrium model.

THE LANGUAGE OF STATISTICS

The concepts discussed here mean that values for the
coefficients of a straight line which by a specific criterion

"best fits" the points plotted in the scatter diagram must
be calculated. A widely-used method is available in the
so-called least squares technique or criterion. The *least
squares criterion* specifies the "best fit" to be the line
that passes through the mean values of the variables on
the X and Y axes *and* that minimizes the sum of the squared
distances between the line and the points in the scatter
diagram. Consider this matter in some detail. In fitting a
line through the points in a plane, there are two coefficients
to be determined, namely, the coefficients *a* and *b* in the
equation $Y = a + bK$. In the least squares procedure it
is assumed that the line will pass through the point whose
coordinates are the mean value of X and mean value of Y.
Thus in Figure 4.5 it would be assumed that the line would
pass through point A. Given only the point defined by the
pair of means, there are an infinite number of lines
capable of passing through the point. However, only one
line of a given slope will pass through such a point.
Thus, the choice of the line comes down to the problem
of finding the slope of the line that passes through the point
defined by the means and at the same time that "best
fits" the remaining points. A measure of the degree to
which these points "fit" can be seen by use of a concept
that is similar to the concept of the standard deviation.

Standard Error of Estimate

In the previous section it was noted that the standard
deviation provides a description of the extent to which
individual observations tend to depart from the mean
value of the variable. It is possible to compute, in a very
simple way, a very similar index of the extent to which
the individual observations tend to fall along a line passing
through the mean values of X and Y in the corresponding

scatter diagram. This index is called the *standard error of the estimate.* It is computed from the following formula:

$$s_{y \cdot x} = \sqrt{\frac{\Sigma(Y - Y_c)^2}{N}}$$

where x is the observed value, Y_c is the value of the corresponding point on the line, and N is the number of observations. It may be noted that the form of this equation is identical to the form of the equation that describes the standard deviation as the square root of the arithmetic average of the squares of the deviations. The index may also be interpreted in a fashion similar to that of the standard deviation. It places similar limits on those values of Y expected to occur with a given X.

But there is implicit in the measure of error chosen, $\Sigma(Y - Y_c)^2$, a criterion for the selection of the slope of the line that is the least squares criterion. The slope may be chosen so that the sum above is at a minimum. A loose but enlightening interpretation of the criterion is as follows: The errors (differences between the values on the line and the actual values) are a function of Y_c such that $U = Y^2 - YY_c + Y_c^2$, where Y again represents the fixed observed values and Y_c is a value that will vary with the choice of the slope. But the shape of the curve relating E to Y_c is as depicted in Figure 4.6. In a fashion similar to that used to find the maximum value for total revenue for the mineral spring operator, the value of Y_c that corresponds to the minimum value of E may be found. According to the least squares criterion, the value of b must be chosen so that

$$b = \frac{XY - N\overline{X}\overline{Y}}{X^2 - NX^2}$$

Given the value of the slope and the point corresponding

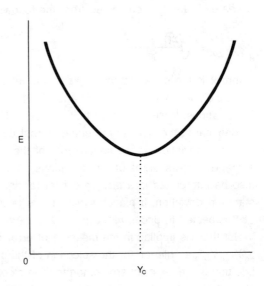

Figure 4.6
Least Squares
Error Function

to the means, the value of the intercept may be computed
from

$$a = \overline{Y} - b\overline{X}$$

Up to this point an intuitive interpretation of the
correlation coefficient growing out of the interpretation of
various scatter diagrams has been encouraged. With the
concept of the standard error of the estimate in hand,
it is possible to compute a precise value for that correlation
coefficient. The formula for its computation is

$$r = \sqrt{1 - \frac{S^2 Y \cdot X}{S^2 Y}}$$

It may be noted that the numerator in the fraction under
the radical is the standard error of the estimate and the
denominator in that fraction is the standard deviation Y.

$$r^2 = 1 - \frac{[\Sigma(Y - Y_c)^2]/N}{[\Sigma(Y - \overline{Y})^2]/N}$$

which expression reduces after manipulation to

$$r^2 = \frac{\Sigma(Y_c - \overline{Y})^2}{\Sigma(Y - \overline{Y})^2} = \frac{\text{``explained variation''}}{\text{total variation}}$$

Thus, a second interpretation of the correlation coefficient is provided by squaring it to produce the *coefficient of determination*. The explained variation divided by the total variation multiplied by 100 yields the explained variation

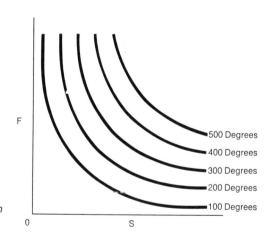

*Figure 4.7
A Production
Surface*

as a percentage of the total variation. To provide an example, a correlation coefficient of .80 means that 64 percent of the variation in variable Y is "explained" by a variation in the variable X.

Return now to the exploration of degree production. Degrees are not produced by students alone, but may rather be thought of as involving students, faculty, and

other inputs in appropriate combinations. These appropriate
combinations may be thought of as resulting from the
resources of educational technology. The process may be
depicted graphically as done in Figure 4.7, which
is a "topographic map" of a production surface. Each
contour line shows the range of student and faculty
combinations from which it is possible to produce a given
number of degrees. Given the "prices" of student and
faculty inputs, a similar cost surface may be constructed
as in Figure 4.8. Each *budget line,* or *isocost line,*

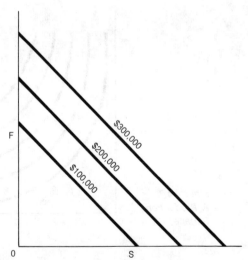

Figure 4.8
A Cost Surface

represents the combinations of faculty and students that
may be "purchased" for a given budget or total cost outlay.
   It is assumed here that the faculty receives salaries
and that the "faculty price" is approximated by that salary.

The "student price" is not to be confused with tuition. Rather, the "student price" may be thought of as the services (including scholarships and fellowships) and facilities that a university must provide (pay to students) in order to keep the student at a university.

The two maps may be used together to show how a university would maximize degree production subject to its budget. Given the budget line $X - X'$ in Figure 4.9, the

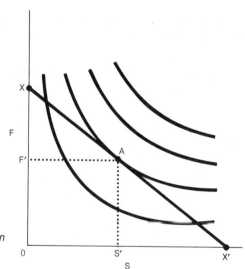

Figure 4.9
The Maximization
of Degree
Production

university would maximize degree production by adjusting faculty and student purchases to F' and S', respectively, since production at any other point would produce fewer degrees at the same total cost outlay. If faculty and student prices varied dramatically between institutions, the depiction of the equilibrium relationship between degrees given (outputs) and faculty and student inputs would have to include an analysis to compensate for those differences.

Assuming that average faculty and student prices do not vary, the production function may be thought of as $D = f(F,S)$. It is quite important here to recall once again the definition of a function as a black box. A particular form for such functions which has found wide use in economics is

$$D = AF^\alpha S^\beta$$

the so-called Cobb Douglas production function, where A, α, and β are constants which are to be estimated from data on degrees, students, and faculty. The particular property of interest to the present analysis is that the sum of the coefficients α and β obtained from the estimate indicate decreasing, constant, or increasing returns to scale according to whether the sum of the coefficients is less than, equal to, or greater than 1. A problem is raised in that our attention has been focused on how to deal with $Y = a + bx$, and not $D = AF^\alpha S^\beta$. But, the reader may recall, $\log_e (F^\alpha) = \alpha \log_e F$, and $\log_e (A \cdot B) = \log_e A + \log_e B$. Thus

$$\log_e D = \log_e A + \alpha \log_e F + \beta \log_e S$$

Ignoring the last term for the moment, it may be noted that the form of the equation is essentially the same as that of $Y = A + bx$. Thus, by substituting the logs of the variables for the values of the variables, the earlier technique applies. If a line of best fit was found for the relationship between $\log_e D$ and $\log_e F$, there would, of course, remain differences between the predicted values of $\log_e D$ on that line and the observed values of $\log_e D$.

These differences could then be related to the values of $\log_e S$ and the value of β computed.

An estimate of the values of the constants made by using data on 83 of the institutions found in Table 4.1 produced the following result:

$$D = .5053 \ F^{.19}S^{.75}$$

The sum of the coefficients is .94, which suggests the plausibility of decreasing returns to scale. A plot of the predicted degree output, together with actual degree output and the value of several of the important statistical words, is found in Figure 4.10.

Now, just what has been accomplished? A comparison of Figure 4.5 with Figure 4.10 reveals that, in statistical terms, the model based on the inclusion of faculty inputs is clearly superior to the model based simply on student enrollments. Visually, the points in Figure 4.5 begin to "fan out" as enrollment size grows large. In Figure 4.10 the points fall more closely along the regression line. As a reflection of this same difference, the coefficient of determination (R^2) is significantly higher in Figure 4.10 than it is in Figure 4.5. In essence, faculty inputs do contribute to degree production.

Focus again on the university as a decision-making entity. In the first model, the only instrument of policy is the scale of the enterprise. The second model indicates that, in addition, the student-faculty ratio is very important. The specific implications of the result may be most clearly understood by the following example.

Suppose that a $50,000,000 budget were available to a university whose production function was that estimated above. Given the budget and a "student price," enrollment, student-faculty ratio, and average costs consistent with the maximization of degree output may be determined. Table

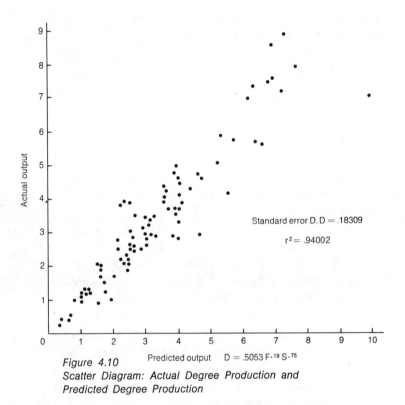

Figure 4.10   Predicted output $D = .5053\ F^{.19}\ S^{.75}$
Scatter Diagram: Actual Degree Production and
Predicted Degree Production

4.3 indicates the results that follow from assuming a
range of plausible student prices. Column 1 contains the
relevant student prices. Column 2 contains
a range of optimal total enrollments. Column 3 indicates
the appropriate student-faculty ratio for that enrollment.
Column 4 indicates the number of students that would be
enrolled for each degree granted (student-degree ratio).
Columns 5 and 6 contain cost per student enrolled and
cost per degree granted.

   The relative importance of the two policy instruments
may now be assessed as follows. A doubling of the size

TABLE 4.3
OPTIONS AVAILABLE TO A UNIVERSITY WITH A $50,000,000 BUDGET[a]

Student "Prices" (1)	Total Student Enroll- ment (2)	Student- Faculty Ratio (3)	Student- Degree Ratio (4)	Cost per Student (5)	Cost per Degree (6)
$ 750	53,200	65:1	8.4:1	$1,000	$ 7,900
1,500	26,600	32:1	7.1:1	2,000	13,300
2,250	17,700	22:1	6.4:1	3,000	18,000
3,000	13,300	16:1	6.0:1	4,600	22,400
3,750	10,600	13:1	5.6:1	5,000	16,500
4,500	8,900	11:1	5.4:1	5,500	30,300
5,250	7,600	9:1	5.2:1	6,600	34,100
6,000	6,600	8:1	5.0:1	7,600	37,600

[a] All values are rounded.

of the enrollment or budget in any of the choices, while
the student-faculty ratio is held constant, would increase
the number of students per degree by about .3. For
example, a doubling of the 50,000 student choice would
increase the student-degree ratio to 8.7:1. Similarly, a
doubling of the scale of the university's enrollments would
have but a modest impact on the cost per degree (about
$300 in the example above).

It is clear, however, that the changes in the student-
faculty ratio have a dramatic effect on degree costs, the
ratio of students enrolled on degrees produced, and on
costs per student enrolled. As may be seen in the table,
a reduction in the student-faculty ratio from 65:1 to 22:1
increases the cost per degree by about $10,000. But,
the decision makers must add, there is a corresponding
reduction in the student-degree ratio from 8.4:1 to
6.4:1.

A greatly oversimplified, but enlightening interpretation
of the decrease in the ratio of students enrolled to degrees
produced is that the time required for the average student

to complete a "four-year program" is reduced from 8.4
to 6.4 years. The decision maker is thus forced by the
model to weigh the costs of prolonging the student's
education against the costs of producing the degree. That
is, the $10,000 increment to the cost of producing a degree
must be weighed against, for example, the earnings the
student must forgo during the additional two years required
by the higher student-faculty ratio.

These observations about scale and student-faculty
ratios seem to have important policy consequences for
both universities and students choosing a university. They
raise a number of questions. What are the technological
factors causing decreasing returns? How may the
technology be most adequately described? To what extent
are part-time students responsible for the decreasing
returns? Are there discernible differences between under-
graduate and primarily graduate institutions? Can the
assumptions about factor prices be said to hold true across
the population of universities? All these questions and
many others would have to be answered before the model
could be of use to policy makers.

There are unquestionably many points of view from
which a university may be treated, and the model
constructed above is only one of them. The importance
of this model is not the particular result produced. It
does illustrate, reasonably well, the complementarity of
model construction and statistical work. The analyst
is not left to speculate endlessly about how it is that
things might work. Nor must the analyst wander through
masses of statistical data in search of meaningful
conclusions. The adoption of the particular tools of thought
limits the intellectual liability incurred and at once provides
a set of guidelines for evaluating the work of others. The
modest confirmation of the hypothesis advanced does
suggest that the model is a first step in a fruitful direction,

and this, in the final analysis, is what the process of
economic thought is about.

THINKING WITH CHAPTER 4

The caricature of the economist is finally complete. Many
of the assumptions used in the process of building it
will have to go unexamined, but the reader should now have
a fledgling's grasp of what economists do. Institutional
description is followed by institutional modeling, statistical
description, and statistical testing. The process recycles
as new insights are gained and new questions are raised.

The reader is urged, now, to set about testing some
of the models that he constructed after reading the
last chapter. As it would not pay to carry out the full set
of calculations set forth for each model, it would be better
to rely on scatter diagrams and tables of classification to
help decide which are worth serious pursuit. The primary
concern is, once again, to acquire a sense of the
meaning of the terms to which the reader has been
exposed and some of the abilities required to use those
terms.

5

on
relevance

THINKING ABOUT ECONOMICS

*The distress, the very real and generous suffering and
distress of an entire generation of young men and women
is related certainly to the miseries of the Sixties, but it is
not founded in them and will not vanish—when, if ever,
the war ends and the hot summers find cool shade and
the assassinations cease. The "relevance" these students
speak is not relevance to the Huntley-Brinkley Report.
It is relevance to their own lives, to the living of their
lives, to themselves as men and women living.*
                                        —ARCHIBALD MACLEISH*

It has been emphasized repeatedly that economics is a
way of thinking. As a method of constructing and verifying
theories about human behavior, it is, in measure,
divorced from the content to which it is applied. The
contents of economics long pervaded the Huntley-
Brinkley Report. The emphasis in this text has
helped, hopefully, to direct the reader's attention to the
more general *and* more important uses of this way of
thinking.

The concepts discussed in Chapters 1 through 4
will become meaningful to the student only as he
applies them and or/gains a deepening familiarity with
their possible applications. The purpose of this chapter
is to suggest some ways in which the student may
use the ideas set forth earlier to gain a deeper insight
into some of his actions. It is further hoped that the
findings of economists on a variety of matters will become
clearer.

The goal of Chapter 5, therefore, is to deal with one of
those problems that make the headlines and whose
outcomes ultimately shape our lives, and to deal with

*"Revolt of The Diminished Man" (excerpts from a speech delivered
on Charter Day at the University of California), *Saturday Review*, vol. 52,
no. 23 (June 7, 1969), p. 17.

it in a way that utilizes the changes in perspective that
the reader should, at this point, have begun to gain.
Chapter 6 is devoted to a broad overview of economics
and a description of a possible approach to the literature
of economics.

The child who is disturbed, but unable to identify the
source of his irritation, is a familiar figure. It is assumed
that, somehow, with maturity, the individual will be able
to pinpoint the causes of his problems with increasing
precision and thus deal with them more effectively.
It is surely true that the "school of hard knocks" provides
valuable lessons—lessons that are hard to come by in any
other manner. However, as numerous economists,
operations researchers, applied mathematicians, and
others have learned, the ability to lament the irrelevant is
not limited to children.

The discussion of problem perception has produced a
small corner in the literature of management science
dealing with the "wicked problem." Managers are depicted
as telling operations researchers to solve a particular
problem—one defined, say, as an inventory problem.
The wicked problem arises when the operations researcher
learns that the "inventory problem"—one that he *is* able to
solve—is but the "growl" of a much larger problem that
he may or may not be able to "tame." Does he simply
solve the inventory problem, accept the smiles and pay
increase that come with the solution, and go on to the
next problem? Or must he tell the manager about the
larger problem and accept the good or ill consequences
bound to arise from making *that* decision?

The ability to develop multiple perspectives on a given
problem is necessary in isolating wicked problems. It also
is of considerable assistance in living with decisions of
the second type. The following section will, perhaps,
illustrate both points.

WAR AND ECONOMIC DEVELOPMENT

It is currently fashionable to look upon the United States and some of the other nations of the developed world as being torn between defending the cause of freedom of choice in the rest of the world and solving their own numerous and difficult domestic problems. The decision to be made by the nation is, thus, whether to continue high levels of defense spending *or* initiate domestic programs for the alleviation of poverty, pollution, resource development, traffic congestion, and so forth. It can be said, therefore, that lurking behind this well-known resources allocation problem is, perhaps, a wicked problem of the type discussed above.

There have always been situations of minor conflict among the developing nations of the world. Most recently, India and Pakistan, Israel and Egypt, Lebanon and Jordan and others have fought one another. In many instances these incidents have involved the intervention of major powers. In the cases of Korea and Vietnam, the United States has felt its interests sufficiently threatened to decide to intervene with a massive response.

In Chapter 2 the fictitious student might well have found the economic explanation of the Crusades—a possibly convenient instrument for coping with an imbalance between the food supply and the number of people needing food—disturbing. Could an alternative view of wars of economic development, one that might place them in a different light, exist?

In Chapter 3 it was observed that it never pays a pair of duopolists to fight. Situations that on the surface involve conflict may, in fact, simply disguise a highly rational cooperative venture that *could not* have taken place without the apparent conflict.

We do not intend, in this section, to model fully such a

situation; rather, we shall apply loosely that important
conclusion of theorizing in economics in order to
produce an alternative perspective on the role of war in
economic development. The outcome will probably prove
as disturbing to the reader as it was to the writer, at first
glance. Upon further consideration, however, it may also
have the merit of forcing the reader to view, with a new
perspective, what is now an old problem.

FIGHTS REVISITED

A short review is in order. In the discussion of Chapter 3
it was observed that there is a single level of output at
which the mineral-water producer would maximize dollar
revenues. The level at which that output will occur is
dependent on the behavior of the consumer of the water.
If the consumer of mineral water decided to purchase
more water at every possible price, the producer's output
would rise. If he was willing to buy less at every price,
that output would have to fall, or else the producer would
not be able to maximize revenue. The presence of one
or a few competing producers would not change the
profit-maximizing output. Disagreement among foolish
producers might engender a price war, but two or more
wise and amiable producers would work out a cartel
agreement to share the returns from the profit-maximizing
output. Historically, producers have developed a wide
range of ingenious devices to assist them in maintaining
such agreements. Experience with such models has
produced numerous interesting observations on collusive
behavior. These include (a) the rewards to be gained
by collusion are very great and, therefore, a few producers
will usually work something out, and (b) appearances
are deceiving; what *appears* to be warfare may, therefore,
well be collusion in one of its many guises.

Suppose, in the spirit of the preceding, that the leaders
of two adjacent countries were to come together to discuss
ways of promoting the economic growth of their respective
domains. Suppose further that they are by nature kindly,
humane, and gentle leaders who strongly prefer
"brinksmanship" to actual combat. They can thus perceive
of war as just around the corner, but would prefer never
to actually *go* around that corner. In what ways might
they conclude that such a "gentle war" could produce
certain direct and otherwise unattainable benefits?

Consider the question first from the perspective of the
internal affairs of the countries themselves. The maintenance
of a large standing army in a small country can be seen
as having certain nondefense side benefits in which these
leaders might express an interest. The benefits may be
divided into those that accrue to the individuals who are
in the army and those that the nation at large
derives from the "appropriate" use of the army.

A large fraction of the populations of the developing
nations are engaged primarily in subsistence agriculture.
The agricultural methods used require little in the way of
the skills needed in a highly industrialized economy.
Agriculture can proceed with a relatively illiterate, unskilled
labor force. During the term of the draftee's service, a
number of things can be done to prepare individuals for
participation in a labor force requiring distinctly different
skills. Literacy training can be undertaken. Individuals
may be exposed to work schedules similar to those in the
industrial labor force. Particular job skills having direct
civilian counterparts may be developed. Direct experience
and information may be used to acquaint individuals
with the nation as a whole. Birth control, personal health,
and elementary medical information may be similarly
transmitted to individuals in whose home communities
such information is not available. A national army under

certain circumstances may reduce tribal animosities and
aid in the nationwide adoption of a common language.
In summation, in the absence of a well-developed system
of elementary education and vocational education, certain
of the educational goals of the country may be achieved
by a system of military conscription.

A similar catalog of potential benefits may be developed
for the nation as a whole on the assumption that the army
is brought into existence by—but not used for—its
apparent purpose. If dispersed, the army might take the
place of a large and expensive local constabulary. The
constant replacement of soldiers might reduce, somewhat,
the coercion and corruption that often accompanies the
development of a more permanent police organization.
The absence of prime males from their homes and the
birth control training that they may be receiving can help,
in a significant way, to reduce population growth. Soldiers
who are not actively fighting may be used in a wide range
of domestic projects which can increment the stock of
social overhead capital. In other words, roads, dams,
deep-water harbors, airfields, public buildings, schools,
and other primarily public facilities may be constructed
using the conscripted and otherwise relatively unproductive
labor force. To the extent that the duration of the threat
of war is utilized to develop nationalistic feelings in the
population at large, levels of savings and personal sacrifice
may be induced in consumers, which in very poor
countries, might not otherwise have been
attainable.

Consider now *small* (underdeveloped) nations with
respect to the rest of the world. The occasion of the threat
of war may be used to extract support from the developed
nations whose value systems the small nations are willing to
espouse. In recent times, the United States and the Soviet
Union have been prodded into providing substantial

military and economic assistance to such small countries. It may, of course, under some circumstances, serve the purposes of the *larger* (more developed) nation to engage in even more extensive activities.

The use of war in the fashion discussed above entails obvious and important dangers. The chief danger may lie in the possibility that the large supporting nations will become nationalistically involved to the extent of turning the "gentle war" of development into a real shooting war, as was the case in both Vietnam and Korea. In a direct sense, the relation of the small nation to a large nation is not unlike the relation of the potential competitor to that of the original mineral-water producer. By threatening to adopt opposing ideologies (threatening a price war), to restrict raw material flows, and to take opposing political positions, the small nation may pose real problems to the large nation. Such a threatening stance toward a "monopolist" *should,* by the profit-maximizing calculus, produce payoffs, just as the original mineral-water producer should be willing to pay fairly handsomely to prevent the entry of his rival.

Since, on the one hand, the threats of war are real and, on the other hand, the dangers of war are real, the large nation is indeed faced with a wicked problem. What is worse, at certain times the war may provide a range of measurable benefits to the large nation itself. If the threat from the small nation should come during a time of lagging employment, high juvenile delinquency, and other disquieting economic and social events, there may be a real temptation on the part of the large nation to reap some of the benefits of a large standing army including a goodly number of those discussed above. The large nation too, may seek to train its young folk in the discipline of the industrial labor force, move underemployed

individuals from the agricultural sector, advance literacy
training, and so on.

Possible Policy Conclusions

The reader is now in a position to consider questions quite
different from those usually considered in a discussion of
Vietnam or similar involvements. *Given* that a major nation
is vulnerable to threats from the developing nations, and
given that there are considerable benefits to be measured
along with the potential costs should escalation of the
conflict occur, *what alternative instruments can be developed
to pursue those same self-interests?* What levels of
foreign aid would be required to buy off the developing
nations? Could such levels be sustained by the developed
world until such times as the threats disappeared?
Could such an incredible program ever receive the
necessary political support from the peoples of the
developed and/or developing nations? What kinds of aid
could insure the integrity of the domestic culture? How
would the small nations react to such programs if they
were offered them? Is massive aid the only alternative to
war? What are the priority rankings for goals within such
programs?

The reader's emotional reaction to the preceding
discussion is undoubtedly mixed at best. Perhaps outrage
at the apparent callousness of the view developed,
mixed with mild depression that the point of view might
nevertheless be valid, may capture some of the flavor of
those feelings. If such feelings are present, perhaps
the reader has just been introducd to a perspective different
from that which he had before reading this analysis.

Economists do not all produce perspectives so clearly
at odds with the conventional wisdom as the view
outlined above. Yet most share in an ability to produce

different perspectives of various individual and collective problems. In confronting these ways of thinking, the reader is faced with a wicked problem of his own.

The reader may choose to remember the facts and arguments that confront him or her in the pages of books and journals. Alternatively, the reader may seek to develop the capacity to apply the conceptual structures on the basis of his own experience in a way that will be stimulating. If a choice is made in favor of the first approach to economics, the reader will soon weary of the task. If the choice is made in favor of the second approach, the reader will soon see that the basic unity of economics is not its subject but its way of perceiving the events of the world. There will truly be room for the reader to quibble and argue about the findings of the economist. However, the best of these arguments will display the promise of economics properly understood. Economics promises *only* a different way in which to look at the events that are of interest to the reader.

A choice in favor of the second approach is not without its perils. In hopes of improving the probability that the reader will survive the trek, the following chapter will attempt to provide some guidelines for dealing with the literature of economics.

6

the
literature
of economics

6
the
literature
of economics

As discussed in the introductory chapter, the literature of economics is the output of economists. It is a rapidly growing literature, and as it grows it changes in response to the changing problems of society. The purpose of the present chapter is neither to attempt to explain the relations among the growing number of subdivisions in economics or to provide a mapping of the bibliography. Some introductory textbooks do an admirable job of the first task; a very helpful volume in alerting the reader to the literature in the field is

Ralph L. Andreano, Eva Ira Farber, and Sabron Reynold, *The Student Economist's Handbook.* Cambridge, Mass., Schenkman Publishing, 1967.

The purpose of Chapter 6 is to reduce the reader's surprise at what he will find when beginning to browse through the literature itself. The *Journal of Economic Literature* will prove to be a widely available source in which to begin browsing. That journal contains short abstracts of many articles recently published in a wide range of journals which are commonly read by economists and in which their works appear. These abstracts will help the reader to find quickly articles on a range of possibly interesting topics and get some feel for the range of works that are available. The next section is intended to help the reader to identify the analytic concerns of economists from those abstracts.

STYLES OF ANALYSIS

Keeping in mind that each economist works at the problems that concern him in his own way, the discussion of Chapters 1 through 4 does allow a broad description of economists according to their analytic concerns. Each

of the approaches is quite as important to the development
of economics as a discipline as the others. However, not
all are equally as easy for the neophyte to grasp.

The model building economist is a latecomer to the
scholarly scene. His arrival only increases the importance
of descriptive activity carried on by many economists
and other social and behavioral scholars. In fact, the
construction of models from misleading institutional
descriptions can only lead to either misleading conclusions
or, what is more likely, hypotheses that fail elementary
tests of their validity. These portions of the literature of
economics will be easily recognized by the reader and
need no further discussion.

If careful narrative descriptions are essential to the
construction of institutional descriptions and, hence,
institutional models, these models cannot be tested without
reference to careful statistical descriptions. An excellent
introduction to the brand of statistical description useful to
model builders is found in the early chapters of

> Edward J. Kane, *Economic Statistics and Econometrics.*
> New York, Harper & Row, 1968.

A healthy respect for the perils awaiting the unwary
user of statistical data is available in

> Oscar Morgenstern, *On The Accuracy of Economic
> Observations.* Princeton, Princeton University Press, 1963.

A volume that will delight those who would construct
models of almost any kind of behavior is found in

> Eugene J. Webb, *Unobtrusive Measures: Nonreactive
> Research in the Social Sciences.* Chicago, Rand
> McNally, 1966.

The literature of economic theory is the workshop of
economics. Something of the ubiquitous nature of the

simple monopoly model has been seen in this volume. There are other conceptual structures in the literature of economic theory (both micro and macro) that have proven useful in the attempt to understand a wide range of problems.

Excellent volumes dealing with the standard models of these areas, in a way that should be comprehensible to the reader, are widely available. However, a mild note of warning is in order.

Chapter 1, the reader will recall, might be paraphrased to say that microeconomics and macroeconomics are dialects of the "language of science." A look at the terms of the broader language is available in

R. E. Emery, *Systems Thinking*. Baltimore, Penguin, 1969.

But lest the arrogance of our scientific tradition overcome us, it is well to observe that there is much to learn from other "scientific" traditions, especially when those traditions relate to human behavior. The reader is directed to

Claude Levi-Strauss, *The Savage Mind*. Chicago, University of Chicago Press, 1966.

As Levi-Strauss clearly points out, there are other rational structures and theoretical "ways of thinking" beyond those that underpin the Western scientific tradition.

The role of the language of mathematics has meant that much effort is expended by economists to determine functions that have properties useful in working with decision-making models, improving their ability to test hypotheses, and carefully defining the ways in which mathematical and statistical tools interact. The following volume covers very well the most important mathematical tools in current use

Alpha C. Chiang, *Fundamental Methods of Mathematical Economics.* New York, McGraw-Hill, 1967.

The volumes and styles of analysis discussed above will prove useful reference works to the student who seeks to pursue the several dimensions to ideas commonly found in studying the works of economists. There remains, finally, the task of developing an approach to particular works of interest to the student.

READING ECONOMICS

It must be said that there is no substitute for continuing communication with other individuals working on similar problems. Several points of view are better than one. In the course of discussing a given work, several points of view are easily generated in a working group.

Reading economics, unlike some other reading, is a paper and pencil business. The reader is as likely to be informed by his own efforts to understand a particular problem as he is likely to be informed by the efforts of the author he is reading. Most novels or short stories are designed to be read from beginning to end. Some articles in economics can be read in that fashion. Others, especially those promising to deal with institutions interacting with one another, can be approached more profitably by the reader in somewhat the same way in which the problem was originally approached by the writer of the article. That is, the reader should go through the the article once, lightly, to collect something of a rough institutional description. Next, the reader should consider any items that are candidates for inclusion or exclusion in such a description. Third, a simple model of the mineral-water producer sort discussed in Chapter 3 should be constructed. Finally, a set of policy conclusions should be derived, and the matter of testing should be considered.

There are two advantages to such an approach. First, the reader makes each reading an exercise in the ability to utilize the tools developed in the first four chapters. Second, the reader will develop a point of view from which he will be able to analyze and criticize the work under study. Finally, the reader will again be reminded that reading in economics is not a search for truth. It is, in fact, a search for relevant points of view.

7

economics:
a systems
perspective

The previous chapters concentrated on developing the concepts by which economists examine and attempt to predict the behavior of decision makers. The student was introduced to the rather different ways of thinking that those concepts make possible. In Chapter 1 the "systems perspective" was briefly discussed. It was pointed out there that the concepts of the systems language are a complimentary language capable of providing yet another way of looking at many of the events and relationships with which economists are concerned. In the present chapter, discussion will return to the systems perspective.

In this chapter, a broad, greatly oversimplified, largely descriptive, and somewhat speculative overview of the workings of the U.S. economic system will be provided. The purpose of the overview is to orient the student to a range of the concepts that further reading in the literature of economics will most certainly turn up. In effect, a kind of mental "hat rack" that will help in the further organization of thoughts about economics and, perhaps, a few other matters will be offered.

We will take the approach of suggesting how the reader's own home town might be studied. The very simple four-systems discussion of Chapter 1 will be

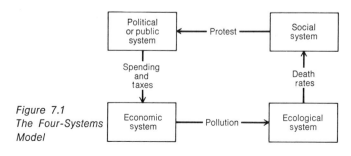

Figure 7.1
The Four-Systems
Model

expanded to give the student a rather detailed set of
questions that can be used to tell him why his
hometown is the way it is. As illustrated in Figure 7.1 and
discussed in Chapter 1, the four systems interact in only
a simple one-directional way. As this chapter will point
out, there are many other simple and direct connections
between these black boxes that are of considerable
importance. Consider first the ecological system.

THE ECOLOGICAL SYSTEM

Ask the following question about the place where you live:
Why do people live here? Were farmers first attracted to
it by the quality of its soil, its rainfall, and its moderate
temperature? Were mining and/or lumber companies
attracted by the richness of its mineral deposits or the
abundance of its timber resources? Did its proximity to
water flows, the inland lakes, or the oceans make it an
easily accessible place through which to transport
goods and raw materials, or is it a place with relatively
abundant water power for mills? Was it a natural harbor
or a way station along a great transcontinental route?
The chances are that one of these questions will lead to the
historic beginnings of almost any hometown.

Historically, the ecological system was a black box that,
with few exceptions, provided outputs in abundance and
there was little need for man to be concerned about the
inputs that the system derived from somewhere else.
Man's presence, like the presence of one more firm in a
highly competitive industry, made little difference. Water
flows, rainfall, and energy from the sun entered most
small ecological systems unimpeded. Unending, if
occasionally disturbed, nutrient cycles were established in
which plant, animal, and human populations grew and
perished in accordance with their compatibility with the

outputs of the particular environment in which they
chose to attempt to survive.* That is, the United States
was a largely agricultural economy with an abundance of
those natural resources essential to the sustenance of
that economic system. The first waves of migration in
this country came about, in large part, as a response to
relative changes in that abundance.

Our mastery of technology has seemed to release us,
at least partially, from a dependence on simple local
ecological systems. In particular, our mastery of the use
of carbon and atomic fuels has, in the short run, allowed
man to "adapt" to virtually any ecological system. But,
as the map in Figure 7.2 strikingly illustrates, the nature
of our dependence has changed somewhat. As may be
seen from that map, the major U.S. cities (over 100,000
in population) that have grown and flourished over the
past two centuries have been located on the banks of
major rivers, almost without exception. That is, the rivers
have (a) supplied transportation for goods, (b) been
converted to energy resources, (c) washed and cleaned
U.S. cities, and (d) provided coolants to dissipate the
heat accompanying our manufacturing processes.

Man can, with little difficulty, locate energy-producing
facilities anywhere. The fuels required to power them may
be transported where needed. Via transmission lines, the
energy produced at these stations may be distributed widely.
While our need for water is much greater than our need for
energy, our mastery of the availability of water is not nearly
so complete, nor is its role and our need for it even well
understood. As the *Scientific American* article referred to
below indicates, the nutrient cycle is a very complex

*For a complete description of the nutrient cycle in one ecological
system see F. Herbert Borman and Gene E. Likens, "The Nutrient
Cycle of an Ecosystem," *Scientific American,* vol. 222 (September 1971),
pp. 92–101.

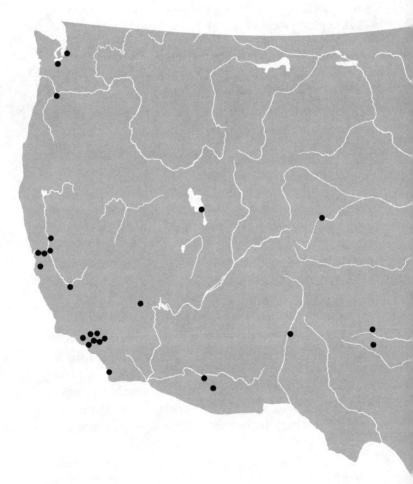

Figure 7.2
The Location of Major American Cities

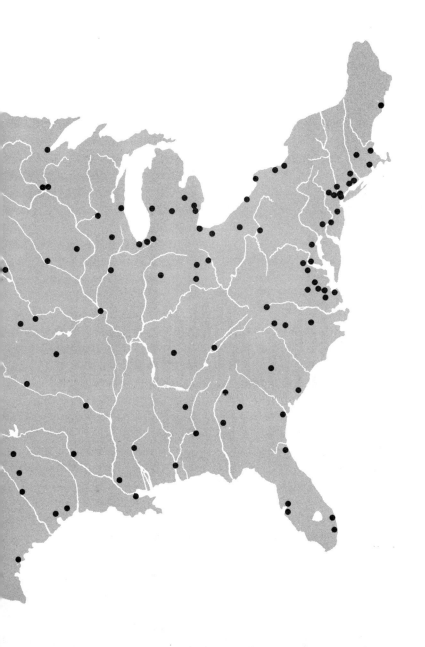

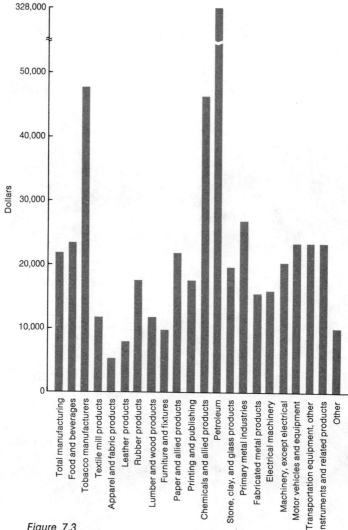

Figure 7.3
Capital Invested per Wage Earner in Selected Manufacturing Industries, 1963
Source: Data after Paul Biederman (ed.), *Economic Almanac, 1967–1968* (New York: Macmillan, for the National Industrial Conference Board, 1967), p. 276.

business, and when man's economic, social, and political
systems are integrated into the nutrient cycle, it is clear
that research lifetimes will be needed to unravel its
complexities.

We shall, then, continue to rely upon water resources
to perform their many functions. Indeed, as the extent of
our reliance becomes clear through research and the
pressure of further development, certain extravagant
uses will become intolerable.

Economics and Ecology

The nature of the immediate dependence relationship
between the economic system and the ecological system
is a simple one. Technological progress has meant
the increasing replacement of human labor with *plant*
and *equipment*. The extent to which *capital* or *capital
goods*—as plant and equipment are called by economists—
have replaced human labor is visible in Figure 7.3,
which contains the dollar amounts of capital per worker
employed by various manufacturing industries in 1963.
The water resources and energy resources discussed
above are, of course, required to move, operate, cool and/
or cleanse and power this plant and equipment.
Technological progress in the production of goods has
thus brought (a) rapidly growing demands for energy
resources, as may be seen in Figure 7.4 which compares
energy consumption per capita among a range of
developed and developing nations, and (b) a parallel
increasing demand for water resources to carry the
transportation, cooling, cleansing, and other loads of the
increasingly complex economic system.

It is a fundamental premise of this economic system
that capital will be used to produce goods and services.
It is a further fundamental premise that capital and human

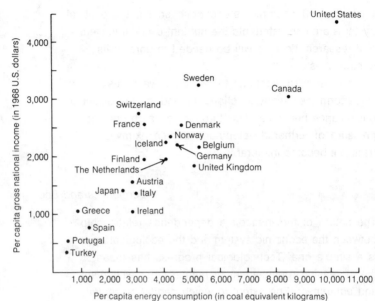

Figure 7.4
Per Capita Gross National Income and Energy Consumption, 1968
Source: Data after *Main Economic Indicators* (Paris: Organization for Economic Cooperation and Development, 1970), p. 136; and *Statistical Yearbook, 1969* (New York: United Nations, 1969), pp. 324–327.

resources are free to migrate to the places that offer them the greatest opportunity. It may thus be observed that the places with relatively abundant water supplies and, to a lesser extent, energy will attract new capital and, therefore, human resources. The expansion of existing places will be limited by the relative availability of water and energy.

The availability of water will depend not only on the absolute volume available, but also on the uses to which the water is put and the relative degradation of that water. For example, it has been recently suggested that the Ohio River will reach the limits of its ability to carry additional heat at some point in the late 1970s. Similarly, many water courses have been polluted to the extent that they are no longer useful even for industrial purposes.

We are led, then, to ask about each community: What are its energy and water potentials? How are its effluents being treated? In what condition is the water by the time it reaches the community? What steps might be taken to restore lost potential? What are the energy resources of the community? What control is the community able to exercise over its water and energy resources? In what ways will the future development of these resources spur or impede the economic development of the community?

THE ECONOMIC SYSTEM

The precise form that additions to capital takes is *investment.* As used by economists, investment refers to the putting in place of new plant and equipment. (Thus, for purposes of the present discussion, your friend's recent purchase of 12 shares of AT&T will have to be excluded.) The investment will be made in a given community by individuals willing to take the *risk* of failure in the market place. Just as the mineral-water operator of Chapter 3 did, they will act as if they seek to make a profit for their troubles. The investment with which we are concerned can be found in agricultural industries, mining, manufacturing and, to an extent, tourism. These are the *basic,* or *export,* industries on which the community depends. The investment may take the form of additions to the capital stock of an existing firm or capital invested in an entirely new venture. The wearing out of the capital stock (the using up of plant and equipment) is referred to as *depreciation.* In the event that depreciation exceeds new investment in a given year, it can be observed that *net disinvestment* is occurring.

Capital, when put in place, will attract, via the labor markets, workers roughly in accord with the total investment and in proportion to the capital requirements

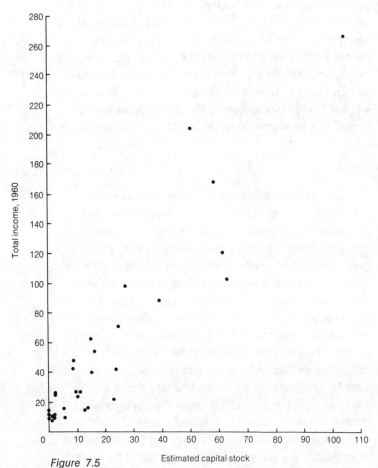

Figure 7.5
Estimated Community Capital Stock and Aggregate Community Income
Source: Data after U.S. Bureau of the Census, *County and City Data Book* (Washington, D.C.: Government Printing Office, 1967). See also source note for Figure 7.3.

per worker found earlier in Figure 7.3. The sale of products of the venture will, if all goes well, earn sufficient revenues to return a profit to the risk taker, wages and salaries to the employees, rents to the landowners, and royalties to the patent and copyright holders. Thus, the economic system transforms land, labor, and capital inputs into outputs that are sold and that return various forms of income to their producers.

In general, the larger the capital stock in a community the larger will be its potential aggregate income, as can be seen in Figure 7.5 which contains a scatter diagram of the estimated capital stock and the aggregate income for a number of isolated U.S. communities. As a general rule, the way in which this income is allocated between

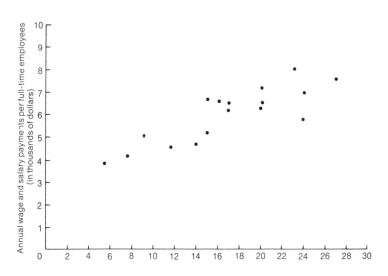

Capital invested per wage earner (in thousands of dollars)

Figure 7.6
Annual Wage and Salary Payments per Employee and Capital Invested per Wage Earner for Selected Industries
Source: Data after Biederman (ed.), *op. cit.,* pp. 82, 276.

capital and wages and salaries is dependent on the amount
of capital that complements each worker. As is shown in
Figure 7.6, the annual average earnings of workers in those
industries that use small amounts of capital tends to be
much lower than the average annual earnings of workers in
industries that use large amounts of capital per worker.

PROBLEMS OF THE ECONOMIC SYSTEM

The attempt to realize the income potential of a
community's factors of production carries with it special
problems. The factors must be evaluated in terms of
(a) the level of market demand for the goods they produce,
(b) the number of firms producing in the same market as
do the firms of the community, (c) the particular character
of the goods being produced, and (d) the impact of
changes in the capital stock on the size, age distribution,
and other characteristics of the population. Chapter 3
discussed briefly the problems of the level of
market demand and the effects that the number of firms
in the market has on that demand. Consider first,
therefore, the effects of the character of the goods
produced by the community.

   Consumer goods can be defined as those goods that
are consumed primarily by families and individuals. These
goods are usually classified into the categories of *durable*
and *nondurable* goods, according to the time period over
which they are expected to yield a service. From the
point of view of the consumer, the decision to purchase
a durable good is one that can be postponed. Thus,
during periods of general economic malaise, consumers
will put off the purchase of goods such as a new
automobile or stove. These delays, of course, will have
a depressing effect on those communities that produce the
durable goods.

The reader will recall from the discussion of Chapter 3 that there is a point on the demand curve for a good that represents the maximum revenue obtainable from the sale of that good in the absence of costs of production. As Figure 7.7 illustrates, for all prices that are above

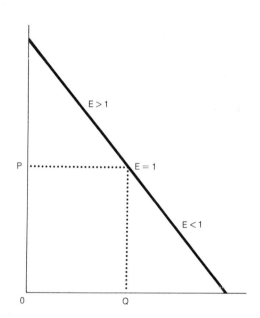

Figure 7.7
Demand and
Elasticity

the revenue-maximizing price, a reduction will bring about a reduction in the total revenue. The region of the demand curve in which a reduction in price or an increase in output will bring about an increase in total revenue is said to be the *elastic* region of the demand curve. The region of the demand curve in which a reduction in price or increase in output will bring about a decline in total revenue is said to be the *inelastic* region of the demand curve. In the elastic region, it happens that an increase in output brings about a less-than-proportional decline in the price, while in the inelastic region, an increase in output brings about a greater-than-proportional decline in the price. Hence, the related changes in total revenue.

The demand for agricultural commodities (and others as well) has been found to be highly inelastic. As a result, a modest surplus of agricultural commodities in a given year can bring about a dramatic decline in agricultural prices and the revenue accruing to farmers.

Many *producer goods* are capital goods, that is, goods used to produce other goods. These goods are subject to yet a third variety of vicissitude. As suggested earlier, a given quantity of capital and a given quantity of labor under a given technology will produce a fixed output. This technological phenomenon may be said to hold for both consumer goods industries and capital goods industries. Suppose that $10 worth of capital is required to produce $1 worth of output in a given consumer goods industry. The producer goods industry that builds capital for the consumer goods industry might normally plan to produce $1's worth of capital each year—in order to plan for the growth of the consumer goods industry—and $1's worth of capital to replace the consumer goods industry capital that depreciates each year. Now suppose that the consumer goods industry stopped growing. The producer goods industry would be operating at 50 percent of *capacity*. Similarly, a 20 percent increase in the demand for the consumer good would result in a 50 percent increase in the demand for the producer goods industry. This amplification of changes in the demand for consumer goods is referred to generally as the *accelerator principle*.

Changes in the capital stock of a community will

demand that the human population that works with that
capital stock undergo certain varieties of change. Without
entering into a full discussion of the interactions between
physical capital and *human capital,* it is possible to point
out several of the more interesting possibilities inherent in
those interrelationships.

The size and age distribution of the human population
in the ecological system of the future will depend on the
current size, age distribution, and *net reproduction rate*
of the population. The *gross reproduction rate* is defined
as the number of daughters who will be born to 1000
women over the course of their childbearing years.
The *net reproduction rate* is defined so that only those
daughters who can be expected to survive until they reach
childbearing years are included. If the net reproduction
rate for a specific community is greater than one, the
community will grow. If the net reproduction rate for a
given community is less than one, the size of the population
in the community will eventually decline.

In a sense, net investment is for capital as the net
reproduction rate is for the human population. That is,
a positive level of net investment is indicative of a growing
capital stock.

It was observed earlier that new capital will attract
additional members of the labor force to the community
into which it is placed. What kind of people will it attract?
Consider the position of an individual worker facing the
choice between remaining in a relatively low paying job
in a stagnant community and moving to another location
where a different—but better paying—type of work might
be available to him if he were willing to undergo the
required retraining. The worker would have to weigh the
costs of moving, the lost earnings during the period of
retraining, and all of the uncertainties of leaving the
community in which he had spent many years against the

benefits of a better paying job for his remaining work years. In general, for persons above, say, 35 years of age, the costs will usually outweigh the benefits. Thus it is primarily the young who *migrate* in response to changes in relative job opportunities.

Young women, of course, are in their childbearing years. It can thus be seen that complex interactions are established between the physical and human capital stocks of the community. Communities in which the capital stock is growing relatively rapidly, for example, will develop two relative bulges in the age distribution of the population. These bulges will result from the influx of relatively young persons and their families. Communities in which net disinvestment is taking place will "age" more rapidly than they would naturally because of the outmigration of younger families in search of superior opportunities.* It is necessary, also, that the potential member of the labor force have the education and training needed to carry on the activities demanded by the technology of the industry he wishes to work in. Thus, changes in the mix of industries in a community will bring about changes in the educational qualifications and skill requirements demanded.

SOME QUESTIONS ABOUT THE ECONOMIC BASE OF THE COMMUNITY

What, then, is the level of capital investment in the basic industries of your community? Does a large or small amount of capital complement each worker at his job? Who are the risk takers of the community? What is the nature of the goods that are produced by the basic producers? Is the capital stock of the community growing

* For a discussion of the ecological growth models that underlie this process see Kenneth Boulding, *Beyond Economics* (Ann Arbor, Mich.: University of Michigan Press, 1969).

larger or is net disinvestment taking place? Is the community dependent on the fortunes of a single industry or is its capital stock diversified into the production of several kinds of goods? What kind of specialized skills, education, and training are required to ably perform the tasks required by employment in these industries? Where does the training occur?

THE ANCILLARY INDUSTRIES

In order to support the basic industry of a community, a number of ancillary industries are required. As may be seen in Figure 7.8, high levels of economic activity are accompanied by high levels of the movement of goods and people from place to place. Thus, the means for transporting goods, people, and raw materials must be provided by a *transportation industry.* Similarly, water and

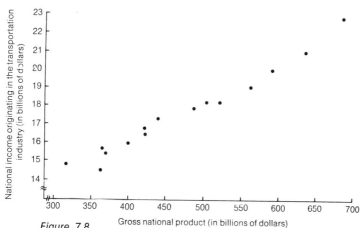

Figure 7.8
National Income Originating in the Transportation Industry and Gross National Product
Source: Data after Biederman (ed.), *op. cit.,* pp. 112–126.

energy must be harnessed or produced for delivery to the place of work, and this gives rise to private or public *utilities*. If new capital investment is to take place, an industrial construction industry must undertake the construction of plants, as is shown in Figure 7.9. It may be noted here that the fortunes of firms in the industrial construction industry follow closely those of firms

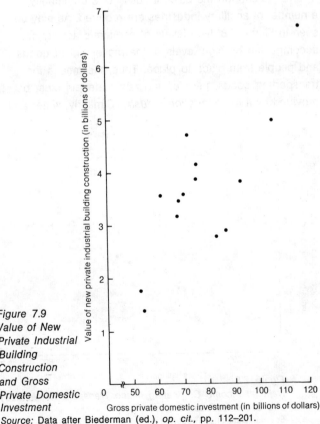

Figure 7.9
Value of New
Private Industrial
Building
Construction
and Gross
Private Domestic
Investment
Source: Data after Biederman (ed.), *op. cit.*, pp. 112–201.

engaged in the production of producer goods. That is, they too are subject to an acceleration principle. Finally, · the investment and production activities require numerous financial transactions, a most important one of which is the *borrowing* by investors of funds sufficient to begin the industry's enterprises or to maintain them through periods of either growth and expansion or difficulty. Thus, the need for *commercial banks* and similar lending institutions is clear.

These few simple observations about the need for ancillary industries lead to a number of interesting questions about your community. The transportation, utilities, and banking industries are heavily *regulated.* This means that the rates they charge are subject to the scrutiny of federal and state regulatory agencies and commissions. What are the effects of the rulings of these regulatory bodies on the services available to the basic industries of your community? Are freight and untility rates high or low relative to the rates prevailing in other communities? Would the rate structure attract investors to your community? What varieties of industry are favored by these ancillary industries? Are they equipped to deal more capably with one variety of enterprise than another?

THE CONSUMER SIDE OF THE ECOLOGICAL SYSTEM

In all, then, the basic industry of the economic system produces incomes for the individuals who work within it and its ancillary enterprises. The total dollar income thus generated in the form of profits, wages, salaries, and rents is a major fraction of what is called *personal income.* The personal income of the community, less the taxes that must be paid on that income, is called the *disposable income* of the community. At least three observations

about a community's disposable income lead to important
questions about the community. First, a major portion
of the disposable income of the community is fed back to
the economic system of the community in the form of
retail purchases. Second, on the whole, a considerable
portion of disposable income is *saved.* Third, the
residential construction industry of the economic system
is dependent upon the disposable income of the
community.

The direct relationship between the disposable income
of the community and the retail sector of the community
suggests that the retail sector will be something of a
reflection of the "life style" of the community. The

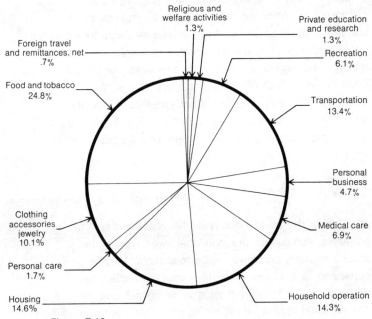

Figure 7.10
Personal Consumption Expenditures by Product Type, 1965
Source: Data after Biederman (ed.), *op. cit.,* p. 382.

reflection may be seen (a) in the distribution of retail spending in the community as compared to the average distribution of retail expenditures given in Figure 7.10 and (b) by considering the distribution of those activities in which an individual might engage in the hours available to him in the course of a year.

Given the retail activity of a community, as it might be distributed on the basis of Figure 7.10, how does your community compare? Is there a greater diversity available or a lesser diversity? Are there a number of relatively small food, clothing, shoe, and similar enterprises, or is there the substantial array of specialty shops indicative of a relatively high level of disposable income in the community?

We all have a budget of 8760 hours to spend in nonleap years. We sleep for about 2900 hours, eat for about 1095 hours and work for some 2000 hours. Do the members of your community allocate their hours for sleeping, eating, and working as specified here? And how do they allocate the remaining hours? What are the effects of that allocation on the nature of the retail sector? What can the retail sector of the economic system tell you about the distribution of those hours?

As mentioned above, a considerable portion of disposable income is saved. The revolution in economic thought that brought about macroeconomics occurred when John Maynard Keynes asked where those savings went. It can be observed easily that if such savings disappeared into coffee cans and under matresses, the retail sector would suffer and the consumer goods industries would, in turn, face flagging demand, the effects of which would reverberate through the capital goods and ancillary industries. Such a frightening possibility always exists, but, as Keynes observed, the bulk of these savings enter the commercial banks where

they may in turn be loaned to investors. The narrative
will return to this observation at a somewhat later point.

As is shown in Figure 7.11, the value of the housing in
a community follows closely the magnitude of the family
income in the community. Roughly, it can be expected
that the value of the house in which a family lives will be
from 2 to 2½ times the family's annual income. What are
the implications for the community of a large stock of

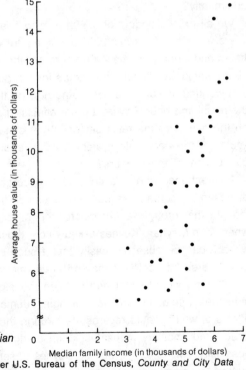

Figure 7.11
Average House
Value and Median
Family Income
Source: Data after U.S. Bureau of the Census, *County and City Data
Book* (Washington D.C.: Government Printing Office, 1967), *passim.*

vacant, dilapidated, or substandard housing? Under what conditions will a considerable amount of residential construction activity take place? If capital produces income and income produces housing, and the housing produced is consistent with the incomes earned, what does the deliberate construction of low-income housing produce?

THE SOCIAL SYSTEM

In the past several sections, the nature of the interdependence of the economic and ecological systems has been considered. In the following section, a range of the characteristic influences and constraints that give shape to the development of the social system will be examined. Our examination will be frankly speculative in nature and designed to raise questions rather than to answer them.

For present purposes, the *social system* will be defined as the black box that receives, as inputs, observations on the behavior of institutions and produces protest, or sanction, outputs on the basis of a "web of rules" that delimits the forms of institutional behavior acceptable to the community.* Ultimately it would be important to specify each of the important rules that a community has developed, the relationship between institutions that it defines, the origins of the rules, the types of behavior that it delimits, the formality or informality of the rules, the conditions under which they would come to be applied. and the intensity with which the resulting sanctions would become manifest.

Our goal is much less ambitious than to even define a

* John T. Dunlop, *Industrial Relations Systems* (New York: Holt, Rinehart, & Winston, 1958). Dunlop's work introduces the concept of the "web of rule."

few of these dimensions to the rules of the social system.
We shall simply ask which of the matters that have been
discussed earlier are likely to affect the specification and
application of the rules of the social system in a particular
community. Thus, from the point of view of individuals,
we are concerned with the geographic distances and
institutional memberships that may separate or join them.
From the point of view of other institutions, it is instructive
to look at the geographic and institutional location of their
leaders. These locations are of primary concern since it
is through the limited interactions of the 8760 hour year
that the transmission, specification, and application of
the rules of the community will occur. Consider now a
range of the variables that will effect the current geographic
and institutional location of individuals within a
community.

The level of income in the community in relation to the
incomes of other communities and the distribution of
income within the community will affect both the geographic
location and institutional memberships of individuals
within the community. Where do the families with relatively
high incomes live? Where is "the other side of the
tracks?" To what extent do church and other organizational
memberships form along income lines? In answering
these kinds of questions it is of interest to note that the
low-income families of a community are comprised of
minority group families, farm families, and families whose
heads are over the age of 65.

The nature of the work place may profoundly influence
location. What are the "normal" hours of work? What
are the seasonal peaks of the industry? As in agricultural
communities, does the technology of the work place
isolate working situations or, as in a factory setting, are
individuals working in close proximity to other individuals?
What are the dangers associated with the work place?

What are the relations of families of the community to the economic history of the community? Are the families among the first to take advantage of the opportunities offered by the area or are they among the recent arrivals who are responding to current increases in the capital invested in the community?

What are the rates at which change is occurring in the community? At what rate is capital being put in place? What are the rates of migration into and out of the community? Is it a community with a relatively large number of persons over 65 so that the death rate in the population will be relatively high in comparison to other communities? At what rates are births, marriages, and divorces taking place?

THE LEADERSHIP OF THE COMMUNITY

The earlier review of the economic and ecological underpinnings of the community makes apparent the critical role of the basic industries in the determination of the income of the community and in bringing about a particular distribution of income. It may be observed that the decisions made by key individuals in the firms that make up the basic industry are likely to affect, profoundly, the course that the economic system takes and thereby affect the social development of the community.

In a similar fashion, members of the banking and legal firms of the community are usually deeply involved in the affairs of the firms of the basic industry as well as in those of householders and retail merchants. The fact of the continuing contact of members of these professions with all segments of the community suggests that certain of their members will be sought as community leaders. Who is the leading banker of your community? On how many boards of directors does he sit? Who sits on the

board of directors of his bank? Which law firms in the
community represent which economic interests?

Who are the leaders of organized labor in your
community? Which industries are organized? How do the
economic fortunes of the trade unions follow the economic
fortunes of the industry?

What are the varieties of economic interest group in
your community? Are there organizations of minority
groups? Is there a Chamber of Commerce? Is there an
Association of Retail Merchants? Is there a local bar
association? Is there a local medical society? Who are the
most influential members of these organizations and
what are their ties to the basic industry of the community?

Finally, it may be asked, how do the geographic and
other organizational affiliations of members of the
community relate to the religious and fraternal affiliations
of the same individuals? Is it "appropriate" that members
of particular kinds of largely economic organizations
maintain memberships in particular service organizations
and fraternal or religious groups?

The web of rules that constitutes the fabric of the social
system can be thought to parallel the web of geographic
and institutional locations that relate to the questions raised
above. Careful mapping of the locational relationships of
the community and the careful observation of the attendant
behavior of individuals would lead to a clearer
understanding of both the implicit and explicit varieties
of rules that govern social intercourse.

THE POLITICAL OR PUBLIC SYSTEM

Who pays the taxes in your community? What are the
tax revenues spent for? The inputs to the political system
of the community include the protests and sanctions
received from the other three systems, the revenues

received from the taxes levied on the constituent institutions of the other systems, *transfer payments* (payments for which no goods or services are received) from other governmental units, and revenues from the sale of the future tax revenues of the community (*bonds*). The outputs of the political system include ordinances, building codes, licenses, and a range of municipal services that, in many cases, are rendered in part through the not-for-profit sector of the economic system. Each of these outputs helps to guide or direct the development of the community.

The ordinances of a community place limits on the behavior of the institutions that make up the community including, of course, the individuals. The particular pattern of the ordinances adopted and the extent to which they are enforced reveal a great deal about the nature of the community. In current practice, *zoning laws* are largely designed to prevent the close proximity of incompatible land uses.* Thus, residential and industrial uses are supposedly separated in most zoning plans. *Traffic ordinances,* in theory, are designed to reduce hazards presented by vehicular traffic flows. The results that obtain in a particular community often differ dramatically from the ideal to which they might conform. Heavy traffic flows are an invitation to retail enterprises regardless of where those traffic flows occur. *Building codes* are designed to insure that the hazards to health and safety presented by faulty wiring, inadequate plumbing, improper construction, and the like are eliminated. How did the particular pattern of codes and ordinances in your community come about? How well are they enforced?

*Ian McHarg, in *Design With Nature* (Garden City, N.Y.: The American Museum of Natural History, Natural History Press, 1969), has argued forcefully and convincingly that a revision of the philosophy of zoning to conform to a range of simple ecological principles would result in vastly superior land-use patterns.

When are exceptions made? Does the overall pattern of
use of these instruments by the governmental unity result
in a community attractive both to capital and to the human
beings who must live in it?

The *licensing* outputs of the political system confer a
considerable privilege on the recipient of the license.
The right to do business as a taxi operator, plumber,
electrician, or other business within a particular community
often carries with it a considerable element of monopoly
advantage. What are the licensing activities in which
your community is engaged? What is the extent of the
economic advantage conferred on the license holder? Are
there provisions for the revocation of licenses? What
provisions insure that the privilege conferred will not be
abused?

REVENUES AND SERVICES

By far the most important output of the political system
is the range of public services provided by expenditures
from the tax revenues of the community.

At the present time, and as Figure 7.12 illustrates, the
tax revenues of the community are largely dependent on
the incomes of the community, regardless of the *tax base.*
The tax base is the objective basis on which taxes are
levied. The most commonly used tax bases are the
properties of institutions, the incomes of institutions, and
the value of goods sold. To specify the *incidence,* or
burden, of a particular tax is to say who finally pays
that tax. As was observed in Chapter 3, the final
specification of the incidence of a particular tax is not an
easy matter. The most commonly used principle of
taxation is the so-called ability to pay principle. The
ability to pay principle holds that taxes should be levied
in accordance with the ability of institutions and

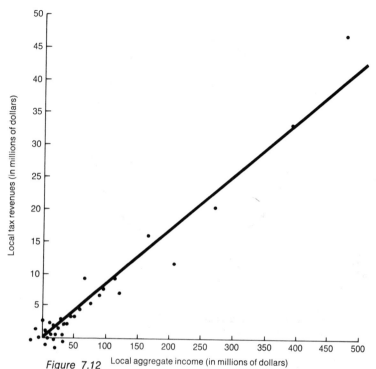

Figure 7.12 Local aggregate income (in millions of dollars)
Local Tax Revenues and Local Aggregate Income
Source: Data after U.S. Bureau of the Census, *op. cit., passim.*

individuals to pay the taxes. The *benefit principle* is also
often utilized, as, for example, in the case of toll roads,
property taxes, gasoline taxes, and hunting and fishing
licenses. The benefit principle holds that the tax should
be paid by the party receiving the benefit of the service.

   Figure 7.13 contains a rough breakdown of the pattern
of expenditures by state and local governments. The
expenditure pattern that obtains in a particular community
will, of course, differ from this pattern. However, by
comparing the pattern of expenditures in your community

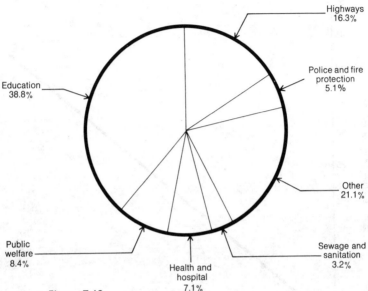

Figure 7.13
Per Capita State and Local Expenditures by Function,
United States, 1965 (Total expenditure by capita, $386.71)

with the expenditure pattern of Figure 7.13 and by studying
the sources of revenues that make possible those
expenditures, it is possible to obtain a rough vision of
the current priorities of your community.

A GRAPHIC SUMMARY

The discussion of the chapter to this point may be
summarized with reference to the reconstruction in Figure
7.14 of the four-systems diagram of Figure 7.1.
As you can see, Figure 7.14 contains a range of the
interactions between the four systems that have been
discussed. As depicted, the four systems largely interact
with one another and there are only minimal connections

to other similar systems or the outside world. In the following sections we shall explore briefly some of the major influences that are brought to bear on the operations of small community systems.

CYCLES AND FLUCTUATIONS

The previous sections provided a very broad overview of the way in which the political, ecological, social, and economic systems of a community interact. In passing, it was noted that there were sources of periodic economic, and thus, to a major extent, social and political, difficulty. The cases in which the tax base of a community rests on an industry subject to the accelerator principle or, as in agriculture, relies heavily on a product whose demand is highly inelastic were noted particularly. The economic system of a community can be a source of difficulty for the community in many other ways. The failure of businessmen to correctly anticipate a set of changes in the tastes of consumers, a prolonged strike, and the depletion of a major natural resource are only a few of the kinds of events that may have consequences that are difficult for a community to face. It would be misleading to conclude our discussion without considering the role that the federal government has come to play in responding to the many sources of economic maladjustment that may face one or many communities at various points in time. While there are many programs designed to allow the federal government to act under particular circumstances, the present concern is to sketch briefly the instruments of monetary and fiscal policy used to intervene in times of economic maladjustment.

The federal role in economic affairs during the past 30-odd years has been defined in terms of three— sometimes conflicting—goals. It has been generally agreed

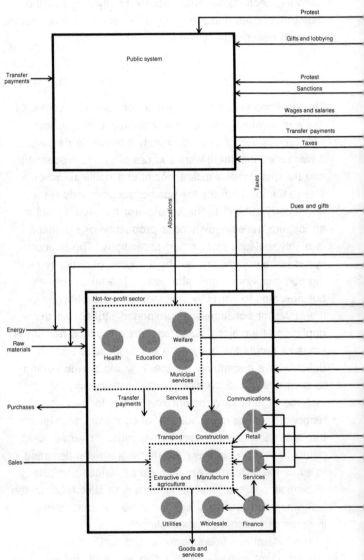

Figure 7.14
The Four-Systems Model

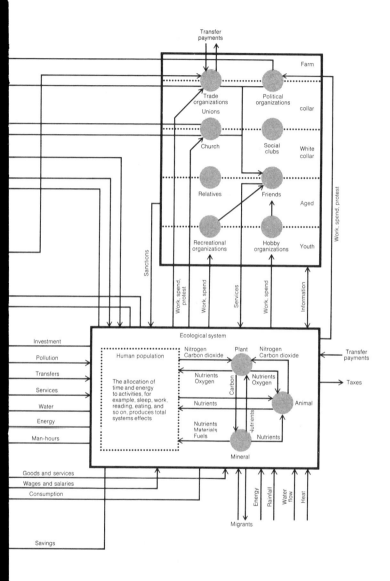

that *economic growth* is desirable and thus the effects of
economic policy have been measured against the rate
of increase of *per capita real income* (by which is meant
the actual market basket of goods available to each
individual). The value implicit in this yardstick is that this
basket should increase annually. The presence of
significant numbers of unemployed persons, of course,
suggests that certain persons are not participating in
the general improvement in living, and thus the effects
of economic policy are considered in terms of the rate of
unemployment. Finally, if the income of an individual
remains constant during a period of rising prices, his
real income is falling. Thus, the third standard for the
assessment of the effects of economic policy has been
the effect of that policy on the rate of the increase in
prices.

FISCAL POLICY

The concept *fiscal policy* refers to the *taxation* and
expenditure activities of the federal government that are
used to effect the objectives outlined in the previous
paragraph. During periods of rising prices, the government
may tax more than it spends and, by thus removing
income from institutions and individuals, reduce the
upward pressure on prices. Similarly, during times of
increasing unemployment the government may spend in
excess of its tax receipts and thereby provide jobs for
human and capital resources that would otherwise remain
unemployed.

It is important to observe that such spending as does
occur takes place in the context of particular communities.
The letting of contracts for specific projects such as
segments of the interstate highway system, defense
systems, post office facilities, parks and recreation areas

brings employment and incomes to particular communities, at least for a period of time. Similarly, the presence of fixed government faciliites may bring incomes to given communities over longer periods of time. Thus, any careful study of a community must measure the costs and benefits that flow to the community as a result of these federal activities.

MONETARY POLICY

It was observed in the previous discussion of the economic system that the banks are recipients of the savings generated by the disposable income of consumers and, in turn, make loans to assist in the process of investment. The activities of the commercial banks of a community are subject to regulation by the Federal Reserve Board (a banker's bank that usually works in harmony with federal government policy makers). *Monetary policy* refers to the range of controls that the Federal Reserve exercises over the commercial banks.

The Federal Reserve banks make loans to commercial banks in much the same fashion that commercial banks make loans to investors. The rate of interest charged to the commercial banks is called the *discount rate*. By adjusting the discount rate downward or upward, the Federal Reserve may enhance or reduce the attractiveness of the lending opportunities available to commercial banks and thus affect the rate of investment spending.

The excess of deposits in checking accounts (*demand deposits*) and savings accounts over the quantity of checks written or withdrawals made during a given time period results in a substantial volume of funds in the "inventory" of commercial banks. Federal Reserve regulation insures that, on the one hand, some portion of these funds may be loaned out and that, on the other,

the commercial banks will not extend themselves beyond
the point of an inability to meet current withdrawals.
By adjusting the *reserve requirements* (that is, the ratio
of the loans made out of the inventory to the inventory
itself) the Federal Reserve may allow the expansion of the
loan activities of commercial banks or force them to
reduce the amount of their outstanding loans.

Once again, the exercise of these instruments along
with the use of the other tools of monetary policy
has its impact in the context of particular communities.
Investment may be stimulated or discouraged. Home
owners may find mortgages either easy or difficult to
obtain, depending on the current policies of the Federal
Reserve. Again, a careful analysis of the interacting
systems of a community must include a provision for
these kinds of effects of federal policy.

IN CONCLUSION

There, dear reader, you have it. One economist's sketchy
view of the way in which economists look at the world.
The oversimplifications used in the presentation have
been extreme, but some of the major forces that act
upon communities and the decision makers who work
within them have been underscored. To ignore them
in attempting to make our society a better place in which
to live would be folly.

Politics that ignore the environments, self-interests, and
interactions of the decision makers and the systems within
which they are contained beg for early failure. For
example, to bring low-income housing to a community
suffering from poverty and unemployment may provide
temporary relief for some of the community's ills. In the
long run, however, the availability of that housing will
simply attract more low-income families. The analysis of

this chapter suggests that the basic problem lies in the quality of the resource base or in the capital stock. Thus, an approach that encourages investment in the tools of industry and education would be far more likely to bring about a permanent set of changes beneficial to society.

Of greater importance, the reader can now perhaps begin to see economics as two powerful and complimentary languages which may be used to deal with the real problems which face society. If so, this volume has accomplished its task.

index